GW00482119

THE ZAEHNSDORFS

THE ZAEHNSDORFS

(1842–1947)

Craft Bookbinders

FRANK BROOMHEAD

PRIVATE LIBRARIES
ASSOCIATION
1986

Frank Broomhead © 1986

Published by the Private Libraries Association
Ravelston, South View Road, Pinner
Middlesex, England

2,250 copies of which 1,000 for sale
S B N 900002 74 3
100 copies bound by Zaehnsdorf
S B N 900002 84 0

Printed in Great Britain by
W. S. Maney, Leeds LS9 7DL
Designed by David Chambers

Contents

5

Illustrations

ILLUSTRATIONS

The device used on the half-title is taken from an impression of a finishing tool in the Zaehnsdorf collection.

Preface

There are few firms of craft bookbinders that can claim an existence of longer than one hundred years. One which can is Zaehnsdorf Limited, founded in 1842 by Joseph Zaehnsdorf. It remained under the direct control of three successive generations of the Zaehnsdorf family for a period exceeding its century; at first under the style of Joseph Zaehnsdorf, and then, as Zaehnsdorf Limited, following its registration as a private limited company in 1913. The company passed from the control of the family in 1947, and, after several changes of name and ownership, it began trading again as Zaehnsdorf Limited, under its present owners, in May 1957.

The era when under control of the family presents a convenient and interesting period for study, and together with the three principals concerned, will be considered in the present essay. The subsequent, but still interesting story of changes made to meet the differing demands of modern times, whilst upholding the cherished traditions of fine craftsmanship associated with the company name, offers scope for a sequel.

Many interesting records and memorabilia are preserved by the company, the earliest going back more than 140 years. Regrettably, these tend to be rather spasmodic, and by themselves do not give a complete history of the firm, nor are there many records of employees or apprentices. The records extant include miscellaneous correspondence, costings for materials and labour for a few specific commissions (with occasional mention of names of workmen employed on the work) for the period approximately 1865 to 1880, testimonials, and various articles from journals, collected under topics such as bookworm, paper-cleaning and bookbinding. There is also an album containing letters of the period 1914 to 1918, received from some former Zaehnsdorf employees serving in the armed forces.

On the basis of the available records, and articles in contemporary trade periodicals, a few perspectives are here presented on the story of one of the better known firms of English bookbinders. It was founded on the skill and perseverance of an immigrant binder, and for over one hundred years adhered to his tenets of fine workmanship, successively under his guidance and then that of his son and grandson. Bindings produced by the firm of Zaehnsdorf are still admired for the excellence of the craftsmanship which they display, and whilst, in the main, their designs rely on the inspiration of the past, innovative essays into more contemporary styles were made on a few occasions. The repair and restoration of books and documents was an important part of the firm's activities, and its principals demonstrated a keen interest in the underlying science. They were also prominent in advocating the desirability of sound binding practice.

1

Joseph Zaehnsdorf

1814–1886

The founder of the firm, Joseph Zaehnsdorf, was born in Pesth (now part of Budapest but then a separate town) in Austria–Hungary on 28 February 1814.* He was the son of Gottlieb Zaehnsdorf, a furrier. After being educated at the Gymnasium in Pesth, he was apprenticed, at the age of 15, as a bookbinder to Kupp of Stuttgart. On completion of his four year apprenticeship, he remained, at the request of Kupp, for a further year; a remarkable event when apprentices in Germany were expected to leave their masters after serving their term. On leaving Kupp he then went to work for Stephan, a leading bookbinder in Vienna, and after a time continued his *wanderjahre* or period of journeyman experience, by working in Zurich, Freiburg, Baden-Baden and Paris. Travel obviously appealed to him, and in addition to widening his craft experience, also helped develop his linguistic ability for which he was noted. Whilst in Paris he had heard that a bookbinder was required in Athens, but before going there he decided to visit London where his brother Charles, who was a manufacturing jeweller, resided. This was in 1837, and following the advice of his brother he decided to settle in London, and there obtained employment with Westley & Co., of Friar Street, Blackfriars. He left in 1839, the year of the 'Struggle' between the men's Trade Society and the large

* Two years are variously quoted for the date of birth of Joseph Zaehnsdorf — 1814 and 1816. The year 1816 was apparently first given in the article in *The British Bookmaker*, iv, (1890) p. 8, which includes a brief account of the early life of Joseph Zaehnsdorf. This served as the basis for many subsequent biographical notices, and the date of 1816 is therefore widely quoted. The obituary in the *Journal of the Society of Arts*, 26 November 1886, which is a useful summary of Joseph Zaehnsdorf's life gives his date of birth as 28 February 1814. This is the date stated on the memorial card printed after his death, which gives his life span as, born 28 February 1814; died 7 November 1886. The evidence is therefore in favour of the earlier, 1814, year of birth being the correct one.

Joseph Zaehnsdorf, senior

employing bookbinders over their employment of what the
men claimed to be an excessive number of apprentices. This
dispute [for details see Howe and Childe, *The Society of
London Bookbinders 1780–1951*. London: Sylvan Press, 1952]
resulted in the three largest London bookbinders, Leighton &
Co., Remnant, and Westley & Co., dismissing all their
employees, stating that they would not employ any men
belonging to the Bookbinders' Trade Society. In all 250 men
were dismissed from these firms. If, as appears likely,
Zaehnsdorf was dismissed from Westley & Co., along with
their other men, because of a long-standing dispute between
the Trade Society and the Master Bookbinders' Association,
one can only guess at the impression this would make on the
new immigrant. Perhaps later it was to influence his dealings,
as an employer, with the unions.

After leaving Westley & Co., Zaehnsdorf then went to
Mackenzie, who was regarded as one of the finest bookbinders
in London. After spending a few years with Mackenzie,
Zaehnsdorf must have thought that he was ready to start
business on his own account, and it is generally accepted that
he did so in 1842. There is some doubt about the exact date of
the foundation of the firm, and uncertainty concerning the
location of its premises in the early years.* In spite of accepting 1842 as the date of the foundation of Joseph Zaehnsdorf's
bookbinding business, it should be noted that his obituary
notice in the *Journal of the Society of Arts* suggests a date of
'about 1840'. A letter dated 26 August 1840, and sent from
Marlborough House, Pall Mall, provides support for this
earlier date, and also the basis for speculation that he might
first have attempted to establish a business other than

---

* Publicity booklets issued by the firm in the 1890s give the date of its establishment
as either 1837 or 1845, but early in the present century the now generally accepted
date of 1842 was being stated. This date is quoted by W. Y. Fletcher in his
contribution on Joseph Zaehnsdorf to the *Dictionary of National Biography*, but which
is inaccurate in several other respects, the dates of occupancy of two business
premises having been brought forward by about ten years. An account of the firm is
given in three articles by Bernard C. Middleton in *The British and Colonial Printer*,
25 December 1953, p. 776; and in *Printing World*, 22 January 1954, pp. 110, 112, 114;
19 February 1954, pp. 213, 214. Contemporary reports of events are given in *The
British and Colonial Printer and Stationer*.

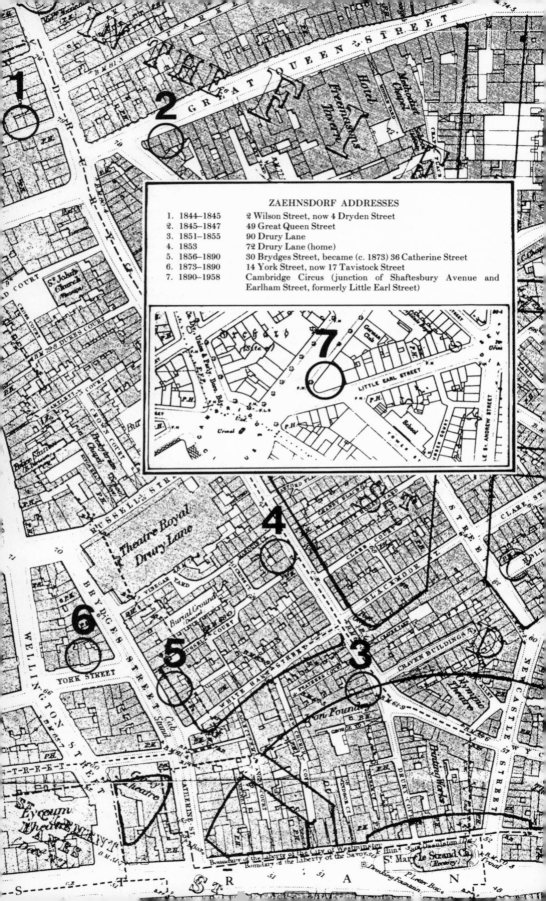

ZAEHNSDORF ADDRESSES

1. 1844–1845   2 Wilson Street, now 4 Dryden Street
2. 1845–1847   49 Great Queen Street
3. 1851–1855   90 Drury Lane
4. 1853   72 Drury Lane (home)
5. 1856–1890   30 Brydges Street, became (c. 1873) 36 Catherine Street
6. 1873–1890   14 York Street, now 17 Tavistock Street
7. 1890–1958   Cambridge Circus (junction of Shaftesbury Avenue and Earlham Street, formerly Little Earl Street)

bookbinding, since the letter states, 'the articles of Toilette Furniture which you left for The Queen Dowager's inspection have been seen by Her Majesty, and I am Honoured with Her Command to acquaint you, that she approves of your industry by devoting your time to the Manufacture of such articles but she does not desire to possess them.' What the articles were which Joseph Zaehnsdorf had left for the Queen Dowager, or what particular branch of industry he had exhibited in their manufacture, is not likely to be known. However, the audacity of the still newly arrived immigrant, in showing his work to the highest in the land, demonstrates something of his character and will to succeed.

It is evident that Joseph Zaehnsdorf, like many others attempting to establish their own business, found the early years difficult. His fairly frequent changes of address are probably indicative of such difficulties, or even if not, they must themselves have created problems for the embryo business. All the known locations for his early business premises are in close proximity, in the Drury Lane/Covent Garden area of London, and it is only from 1851, when the name of Zaehnsdorf begins to appear regularly in the London Directories, that there is any certainty about the addresses. The first of Joseph Zaehnsdorf's binderies was at 2 Wilson Street (now designated as 4 Dryden Street) off the west side of Drury Lane. Middleton, using the evidence of rate book entries, gives the Zaehnsdorf occupancy of these premises as being from 1844 to a date before 15 July 1845. The earliest known Zaehnsdorf binding (which will be considered in more detail later) bears his ticket 'J. Zaehnsdorf, Bookbinder, 2, Wilson Street, Drury Lane'. The first time Zaehnsdorf's name is mentioned in the London Directory is in 1847, when his address is given as 49 Great Queen Street. *The British Bookmaker* of February 1892, referring to R. de Coverly states that he was born on 12 February 1831 and at the age of 14 was apprenticed to Joseph Zaehnsdorf of 49 Great Queen Street. Accepting the accuracy of this statement, and the fact that apprentices were usually bound on, or near to their birthdays, indicates that Zaehnsdorf was at the Great Queen Street address early in 1845. This fits with the occupancy of 2 Wilson

15

Opposite: Map showing location of Zaehnsdorf binderies and outline of the later Kingsway/Aldwich development

17 Tavistock Street, formerly 14 York Street, in 1942, showing
bay window, at street level, as in Zaehnsdorf's time (since removed)
(Courtesy GLC Photograph Library)

Street from a date in 1844, and then a move to Great Queen Street occurring some time before, or less likely, shortly after 12 February and certainly before 15 July 1845. By 1848, the year following his first directory entry, he had moved from the Great Queen Street premises which were then shared between a coffee house and a theological bookseller and printer. No further business address is known for him, nor does he appear in the directories, until 1851. It could have been that, during these years, shortage of work had forced him either to share premises, or to find employment with another bookbinder.

In 1851 his address was given as 90 Drury Lane and he stayed there until 1855, these premises being shared with fringe makers, a carver and gilder, and a gold lace maker. His next address, as given in the directory entry for 1856, was 30 Brydges Street (later to be designated 36 Catherine Street). By this time Joseph Zaehnsdorf was obviously becoming established. On 28 August 1858 he signed a lease for these premises, at a yearly rent of £48, from The Duke of Bedford. On 22 October 1879 he leased the premises for a further term of seven years at an annual rent of £140. In 1873, he also occupied other premises forming part of the Bedford Estate at 14 York Street, Covent Garden (now 17 Tavistock Street). The first directory entry, in 1874, for Zaehnsdorf at this address describes him as a printer, but his venture into this trade must have been short-lived since he is described as a bookbinder in all subsequent entries. York Street had long been associated with bookselling and publishing, having housed at different times, Samuel Baker, H. G. Bohn, and George Bell & Sons. The York Street address had various other tenants in addition to Zaehnsdorf, including successively, a bookseller, a publisher, the Theatre Mission Institute for Youths and Boys, and it also served as a newspaper office. For Zaehnsdorf it was his home and office/showroom, whilst the atelier (so described on his trade card) remained at 36 Catherine Street (formerly, 30 Brydges Street).

Whilst Joseph Zaehnsdorf was striving to establish his craft bookbinding business, mechanisation was being introduced

DUBLIN 1865. PARIS 1867. VIENNA 1873.

HONORABLE MENTION, INTERNATIONAL EXHIBITION 1862.

J. ZAEHNSDORF

ENGLISH AND FOREIGN

BOOKBINDER,

36, Catherine Street,
(Late 30, Brydges Street.)
STRAND, London, W.C.

Zaehnsdorf Business Card, 1873

apace, particularly in the larger binderies, in order to meet the increased demand for books from the new middle class. Although machines were to be beneficial in the long-term, their immediate effect was to result in disputes between the employers and the men being displaced by the machines. The larger binderies, who could better afford the capital outlay on new machines, then had the consequent advantage of reduced costs, and could, therefore, capture a larger share of the available work, to the detriment of the smaller binders. The first rolling machine, to replace hand beating to obtain a solid book, had been introduced as early as 1827 and it was in widespread use by 1830. A blocking press, for titling, to replace hand methods, followed in 1832. These developments were only the beginnings, and by the 1850s the basic mechanical process had been introduced — a folding machine, for folding the sheets as received from the printer; a cutting machine, for book edges; a backing machine, which gives the book the ridges or shoulders where the boards fit; and a sewing machine. The steam engine was now a reliable source of

18

R. Bradford. 59 Holland Park. W.

Honorable Mention
· International ·
Exhibition 1862.

DUBLIN 1865.

PARIS
1867.

J. ZAEHNSDORF

English and Foreign
BOOKBINDER.

VIENNA 1873

LONDON 1874

Office, 14 York St, Covent Garden

Atelier, 36 Catherine St, Strand.

LONDON, W.C.

Removed to Cambridge Circus, Shaftesbury Avenue, W.C.

Zaehnsdorf Business Card, 1890

power to drive such machines, and with further mechanical inventiveness (usually supplied by America) mechanised bookbinding was a reality.

Against this background it was not easy for Joseph Zaehnsdorf to establish his business, but a combination of perseverance, hard work and a sound knowledge of his craft was eventually to bring him success, even though he had to wait nearly twenty years. An indication that he may have been finding regular commissions is given by a letter from the Hanoverian Legation in London, dated 4 May 1861, which refers to 'Mr Zaehnsdorf, Bookbinder to the King of Hanover'. His first public acknowledgement came in 1862, when he received honourable mention at the London International Exhibition. He became a member of the [Royal] Society of Arts in this year. He was awarded medals at the

19

Anglo-French Working Class Exhibition at the Crystal Palace in 1865, at the Dublin Exhibition of 1865, at Paris in 1867, at Vienna in 1873, and at the London International Exhibition, South Kensington, in 1874. In addition to exhibiting at South Kensington, he also organized a special workshop so that visitors might see the actual processes of extra bookbinding.

A first-rate craftsman himself, Joseph Zaehnsdorf demanded high standards from his employees to whom he was a firm, but fair, master. A dispute with the unions in 1872, over his employment of a large number of low-paid German workers, was aggravated by Zaehnsdorf placing an ill-considered advertisement for employees in the *Clerkenwell News*, which stated a preference for non-Society men. As a result, the Amalgamated Committee of the Unions gave an instruction that all members should give notice, and nineteen employees left on 28 September 1872. No doubt these events would remind Zaehnsdorf of his early days in England, and the 'Struggle' of 1839. The loss of these workers, many of whom were skilled craftsmen (their names are given in Appendix A), must have been a setback for the firm, albeit only a temporary one. Joseph Zaehnsdorf must have resisted union pressure over the employment of foreign binders, since the Official Catalogue of the 1874 London International Exhibition carried an advertisement by Joseph Zaehnsdorf offering bookbinding 'by English and Foreign Workmen'. The employment of a number of German binders, several of whom were outstanding craftsmen, continued to be the policy of the firm until the outbreak of the First World War.

When he first came to London, Joseph Zaehnsdorf lived for several years at 6 Frith Street,* Soho, with his brother, who was then single — he married in September 1841. Joseph Zaehnsdorf married twice, and on each occasion gave his address as 4 Gough Street. His first marriage was on 11 January 1845, to Ellen, daughter of William Donovan, a tailor living at 5 Dollington Street, Mount Pleasant, which was close to Gough Street. Ellen Zaehnsdorf died in 1848.

* Now marked with a blue plaque as the death-place of William Hazlitt, the essayist, on 18 September 1830.

PRIZE MEDALS AWARDED

 DUBLIN, 1865.  PARIS, 1867.  VIENNA, 1873.

BOOKBINDING
In the MONASTIC, GROLIER, MAIOLI, and ILLUMINATED STYLES,
In the most superior manner, by English and Foreign Workmen.

JOSEPH ZAEHNSDORF,
36, CATHERINE STREET. (*late Brydges Street*), COVENT GARDEN, LONDON, W.C.

A Zaehnsdorf Advertisement, in the
Catalogue of the London International Exhibition, 1874

Joseph Zaehnsdorf's second marriage, in July 1849, at Trinity Church in the Parish of St Andrew Holborn, where his earlier marriage had also been solemnised, was to Ann Mahoney, then a minor and daughter of William Mahoney, an engineer and also a resident of Dollington Street, but at No. 2. The only child of this union, Joseph William, was born on 1 June 1853, at 72 Drury Lane, the Zaehnsdorf home at the time, adjacent to Joseph's bindery, at 90 Drury Lane.

Joseph Zaehnsdorf received his certificate of naturalization, as a British citizen, on 15 September 1855, (three years after his brother). He died, in his 73rd year, at his home, 14 York Street, on 7 November 1886. He left gross estate valued at £3893. His will, dated 9 October, in the year of his death, bequeathed his gold watch and chain 'which I usually wear' to his son, and four sums of five pounds five shillings [£5.25] to friends for the purchase of mourning rings. Bequests were made to three of his workmen, five pounds five shillings each to Fritz Maullen and to Heimlein, and two pounds ten shillings (£2.50) to Thomas Preston. To his wife he left all his other estate, including the goodwill of the business for her own absolute use and benefit, but with the proviso that whilst ever she carried on the business, his son, Joseph Zaehnsdorf, should be employed in the management and be paid, by monthly payments, an annual sum of £300 providing that the profits should be sufficient to allow such a payment. This will shows the recognition by Joseph Zaehnsdorf of the value to the business of his son, by requiring that he be paid what for those days was a significant sum; there is also acknowledgement of the efforts of his foreman finisher Maullen and foreman coverer Heimlein, both Germans.

The eulogy given at his interment at St Mary's Cemetery, Kensal Green, and reported in *The British and Colonial Printer and Stationer*, on 23 December 1886, provides a telling commentary on the man,

. . . we have gathered here today to pay homage and our last respects to the mortal remains of our much esteemed and lamented Governor, Mr J. Zaehnsdorf. Death has at last released him from a painful and protracted illness. It has taken him away not only from his sorrowing family, to which he was fondly attached, but also from his flourishing and well-established business, of which he was the founder, and which he, through his never-ceasing energies, had succeeded in bringing to pre-eminence.

. . . as a business man, he was of high and unimpeachable character, upright, and straightforward in all his transactions, which won for him the esteem of all his business friends and every one who came in contact with him.

To us, his Employees, he certainly was very strict and particular with regard to our work; but this strictness was always tempered by good-humour, gentleness, and kindheartedness; and these, I can candidly say, were his bright and shining virtues. Having risen from the ranks, as I may term it, like any one of us; from being a working man, he well knew, and never forgot the troubles, anxieties, and cares which befall so many of us in our humble station of life; . . . his advice, his experience, and what is often more, his purse, were always ready and open to assist any one of us who were deserving of it.

2

Joseph William Zaehnsdorf
1853–1930

Whilst Joseph Zaehnsdorf was the founder of the firm, it was under his son, Joseph William, that it was to develop further, and prosper. Joseph William* was educated initially in this country, followed by three years at St Omer, in France. He was then apprenticed as a bookbinder in Cologne for a short time. His period of apprenticeship abroad was cut short by the outbreak of the Franco-German War, and he returned to England in 1870, and completed his apprenticeship under his father. At the time of his father's death in 1886, he was already running the business. *The British and Colonial Printer and Stationer*, after the account of his father's interment, refuted 'an impression that in consequence of the death of Mr Joseph Zaehnsdorf, the business may not be continued as hitherto'; by stating that 'this is a mistake, as Mr J. W. Zaehnsdorf has practically been manager of it for years past. For over sixteen years he has been in sympathetic work with his father, and for the past four years he has had entire management.'

J. W. Zaehnsdorf was establishing his reputation as a bookbinder with an audience wider than just his business contacts. He did much to make known the principles of sound binding practice, and to increase the appreciation and knowledge of fine binding, and he wrote articles and a book of instruction for amateur bookbinders — quite a daring innovation for those days, from someone engaged in the bookbinding trade. He is still remembered for his book *The Art of Bookbinding*, first published in 1880, by his neighbours in York Street, George Bell & Sons, with the author's intention 'to

* A short obituary by E. J. W. Zaehnsdorf of his father, published in *The Bookmart* of 7 November 1930, includes brief details of J. W. Zaehnsdorf's early education and his service in the volunteers.

23

Joseph William Zaehnsdorf, about 1890

give the amateur sufficient knowledge to enable him to avoid such mistakes in his purchases, [gaudy but unsound bookbinding] and at the same time give him as much instruction as will, if his inclination and time permit, enable him to bind his own volumes as his wishes and taste may dictate.' A second edition, with much additional material, was published in 1890, and was intended for the use of the trade, amongst whom the first edition was stated to have had a large sale. Other editions and impressions were published in 1897, 1900 and 1925; a reprint of the second edition was issued in 1967 and again in 1969. This was an important book, being one of the first substantial English manuals on the practice of bookbinding. W. J. E. Crane's *Bookbinding for Amateurs*, was published in 1885 and re-issued in 1903, and in comparison with Zaehnsdorf's book, had a greater number of illustrations, and more detailed descriptions of the processes involved. Zaehnsdorf's book continued to be in demand, in spite of its shortcomings. It was not until 1901 that Douglas Cockerell's *Bookbinding, and the Care of Books*, was published, and for many years the two books gave the only comprehensive survey of the craft of bookbinding — Zaehnsdorf the more traditional trade practices, whilst Cockerell followed the precepts of T. J. Cobden-Sanderson, who had done much to revitalise English bookbinding design in the years from about 1885 to 1893. There is a link, albeit tenuous and indirect, between the elder Zaehnsdorf and Cobden-Sanderson. Roger de Coverly had been apprenticed to Zaehnsdorf, and it was de Coverly that Cobden- Sanderson asked, in June 1883, for his initial instruction in bookbinding.

During 1881–83 J. W. Zaehnsdorf contributed a series of six articles on 'Amateur Bookbinding' to *Amateur Work Illustrated*; these being attributed to the 'Author of *The Art of Bookbinding*'. In the final article, on 'Finishing', he states that this is the branch of bookbinding which the amateur will find most difficult. In concluding the article he offers his readers 'to put them in the right way' should any difficulty arise, and promises a future paper on other matters pertaining to bookbinding. This reference may have been a rather premature one to *The Bookbinder*, of which he was editor for its first three volumes in 1888–90. This monthly periodical changed its name for its fourth and later volumes to *The British Bookmaker*, and became more concerned with trade matters for the remainder of its seven volume life, rather than being, as stated its original sub-title, 'An Illustrated Journal for Binders, Librarians and Lovers of Books'.

In 1886 J. W. Zaehnsdorf spoke to the Annual Meeting of the Library Association, of which he was a member, on 'Practical Suggestions in Bookbinding'.* During the course of this talk, which was printed the next year in *The Library Chronicle*, he mentioned that many bookbinders were waiting for work, and then stressed that good bookbinding depended on the use of the best materials and skilled workmanship. He highlighted the importance of sound sewing with best thread, the preferred use of flexible sewing, and the use of good leather, which are still the prerequisites of a good binding. He concluded by mentioning protective boxes for books, of which he said he had made a study, and then invited inspection of a sample, but indicated that he did not wish to go into the matter fully, as it had cost him time and money which he wished to recoup.

The fire-resisting pull-off box is an example of the inventiveness of J. W. Zaehnsdorf, but the available evidence suggests that he was not very successful with its commercial exploitation. Ten years after his Library Association lecture he was still trying to commercialize the box. The name of the famous bookseller, and friend of the elder Zaehnsdorf, Bernard Quaritch, is connected with practical tests to prove the worth of this invention, and various stories have been told concerning the manner and circumstances in which these tests were made, such that it is worth quoting, in full, the letter from Quaritch:

* George Watson Cole, in his *Index to Bibliographical Papers*, (1933), gives the dates of 1816–1886 to the author. *The Library Chronicle*, (1887), on printing the paper, only gives the author's name as, Mr J. Zaehnsdorf; as does *The Times*, in its report, on 1 October 1886, of the meeting. The lecturer is unlikely to have been Joseph Zaehnsdorf senior, then within six weeks of his death, after a 'painful and protracted illness'. The lecturer, clearly, must have been the son, J. W. Zaehnsdorf. The year of birth, given by Cole, for Joseph Zaehnsdorf, senior, is wrong; it should have been 1814 [see footnote to page 11].

LONDON, 15 Piccadilly, W.   September 30 1896

Dear Mr. Zaehnsdorf

You were present when we tested your leather cases in a large bonfire in my garden.

You recollect, in spite of fire, water and tallow candles the three cases (with books inside) were only damaged, whilst the books were absolutely uninjured.

If your customer wants to hear more on the subject send him to me.

Yours truly
Bernard Quaritch

Further evidence of Zaehnsdorf's efforts to exploit his fire-resisting box is given by a letter, dated 7 April 1897, from Cyril Davenport of the British Museum, who thanked him for the fireproof cases and invited him to the Museum to meet Mr Garnett [Richard Garnett, Keeper of Printed Books, 1890–1899].

J. W. Zaehnsdorf's fire-resisting box was most likely not patentable; however, he did apply for two other patents. In 1888 he was granted a patent, No. 15,936, for preparing photographs and other pictorial cards or mounts for connecting them in a book-like formation. This invention was 'chiefly intended for use by Photographic Amateurs to enable them to keep their Photos as mounted in compact order and clean'. It was the now well-known principle of double hinged leaves. The specification stated — 'the object of my invention is to attach two strips of cardboard to the guard to form two distinct folding places beyond the inner edge of the mount and to make one of the strips, namely the outer one, of greater width than that of the inner one and to perforate said larger strip so that any number of such prepared mounts can be arranged in a superposed manner to any desired height: the perforations, all of which correspond in the larger strips serve for a cord or lace to be passed through to hold all of the mounts in that superposed condition, the two folding places permitting the compilation of mounts to be open at any part without interfering with the lacing at the back'. Zaehnsdorf's Self-Binding Mounts, as they were termed, were manufactured by

Goodalls and each batch was tested for deleterious ingredients before being sent out [an early understanding of the principles of conservation]. The London agents for the mounts being the Eastman Dry Plate Co., of Oxford Street. A later patent application by Zaehnsdorf, No. 2038 in 1893, for preserving the gilded surfaces of books, was abandoned or void, and the application was therefore not printed, and nothing further is known of the proposal. However a tool was cut, which is still in the possession of the company, giving this patent number, presumably intended for impressing on bindings treated by this process.

ZAEHNSDORF'S PATENT
NO—2038

Hand stamp for Zaehnsdorf's preservation
process

The Catherine Street and York Street premises continued to be used after Joseph Zaehnsdorf's death. The future of the bindery, or atelier, in Catherine Street, must have been less than secure throughout the time of the Zaehnsdorf occupancy, since a scheme for a new road to improve communication from Holborn, near Southampton Row, to the Strand, near Somerset House, was first mooted in 1836. Little appears to have been done, other than periodic discussion of the proposal, until 1883, when the Metropolitan Board of Works (the predecessor of the London County Council) concluded that a street from Holborn to the Strand, and also a widening of the Strand, was an urgent requirement. Apart from these external planning developments, increasing trade and the inconvenience resulting from the office and works being in separate, albeit reasonably adjacent buildings, were forcing the need for a move on to Zaehnsdorfs.

In July 1890 they moved to their purpose-built premises, designed by Messrs Rowe and Julian, of Basinghall Street, London EC. These premises were one of the first buildings to be occupied in Cambridge Circus, and were located on a perfect site for their requirements, being a peninsular formed by the junction of Little Earl Street (now Earlham Street) with

Zaehnsdorf's Bindery in Cambridge Circus, 1890
Top: Exterior   Below: Showroom

Two views of the Forwarding Department

Top: the Covering Department   Below: the Finishing Department

Shaftesbury Avenue. This site, slightly less than half-a-mile to the west of the Catherine/York Street premises, had a frontage on Shaftesbury Avenue, towards the north, of fifty-five feet, and on Little Earl Street towards the south, of fifty-two feet. At its western boundary the site faced onto the junction of Little Earl Street and Shaftesbury Avenue, in a curve of some twenty-three feet, at its abutment on the eastern boundary the site was some fifty feet wide.

The British Bookmaker, in its July 1890 issue contained an illustrated article on these premises, based on a brochure* issued by the firm, and on a visit. The ground floor was given over to an extensive showroom and general offices, whilst folding, sewing and collating were carried out in the basement. Windows along both sides of the building gave excellent natural lighting, which was advantageous on the other floors which housed the forwarding, covering, and finishing departments. There was also a leather store. The Cambridge Works, 144–6 Shaftesbury Avenue, continued as the Zaehnsdorf Bindery until 1958. The building is still standing today, with its external appearance little changed from what it was in 1890, and exhibiting a panel of sculptured stone on the front elevation at the lower level of the second floor, showing a binder working at a sewing frame, a device which figured frequently on Zaehnsdorf stationery and in their advertisements.†

For over one hundred years, since its first foundation by Joseph Zaehnsdorf, the firm's binderies had always been sited in the same small area of London, in the vicinity of Drury Lane (see map, page 14). The present-day pilgrim to the sites of the early Zaehnsdorf binderies will find that only two of the buildings, other than Cambridge Circus, are still standing. The building which housed the first bindery, at 2 Wilson Street, is now redesignated 4 Dryden Street, and is still to be seen. No trace remains of 49 Great Queen Street, the site being towards the north-east corner of the present Freemason's Hall. The premises at both 90 Drury Lane and 36 Catherine Street disappeared at the turn of the century, in

* For information about this, and later publicity pamphlets issued by the firm, see Appendix B.
† For the source of this illustration, see Appendix D.

the Kingsway/Aldwych scheme. The site of the Drury Lane premises is now occupied by the pavement in front of, and the north-west corner of Bush House West; whilst the site of the Catherine Street bindery is now occupied by part of the Strand Theatre. The house and office/showroom at 14 York Street, where Joseph Zaehnsdorf died, is now 17 Tavistock Street, and externally, at least above street level, is little altered from those days.

The training of non-trade bookbinders was likely to have created resentment from the unions. De Coverly's shop was probably too small to have union problems over his provision of instruction for Cobden-Sanderson; whilst Zaehnsdorf had shown, on other matters, that he was prepared to take a firm line. Whatever the problems may have been, it is of interest to note that Zaehnsdorf had at least one non-trade pupil during the 1880s who was to achieve fame as a bookbinder, and, to some extent, both as a writer on bookbinding and a teacher — Sarah Treverbian Prideaux (1853–1933). The fact that she was a woman could only have tended to worsen the situation, at a time when there was a clear, and jealously guarded, distinction in trade binderies between the work of the two sexes. 'Women's work', as it was termed, was restricted to the sewing of the sections of the books and headbanding, all other processes including cutting and gilding the edges, covering with leather or other material and titling and decoration, were exclusively in the province of the males.

The Arts and Crafts movement, in which William Morris and Cobden-Sanderson were prominent, had created an interest, and also a demand for instruction, in many crafts during the last decade or so of the nineteenth century. Bookbinding was foremost amongst these, and was considered to be eminently suitable for young ladies, especially of the educated and leisured middle class, to practise. This demand, and the availability of additional space, which could be separated from the main workshops, with J. W. Zaehnsdorf's business acumen resulted in his offering a course in bookbinding. Details of the course are given in an announcement from Cambridge Circus, dated 1 January 1891. Instruction was to be under the guidance of their former pupil, Sarah Prideaux.

The first floor of the new premises had been set apart and was to be fitted out for the students, with a separate door at No. 146 Shaftesbury Avenue. Each pupil was to have a separate bench, press and necessary tools. The course was to be of three month's duration, at the end of which time it was expected that the students would have learnt sufficient to continue working on their own. Instruction was to be given in various details of the trade, including forwarding and finishing, on three mornings of the week, with the workshop open the whole of the day for practice. The fee for the course, including use of materials, was fifty guineas (£52.50). Unfortunately, it is not recorded who, if any, were the pupils enrolled on this course. It can only be assumed that either it never took place, or its success was limited, since no other mention has been made of the course, or its pupils.

The bookbinding activities of Sarah Prideaux ceased about 1904. A collection of articles on various aspects of bookbinding, which she had contributed to several magazines, was published in America in 1903 as *Bookbinders and Their Craft*. The English edition was published by Zaehnsdorf.

Whatever the success of the classes at the Cambridge Circus Works, J. W. Zaehnsdorf's interest in bookbinding instruction continued. *The British Bookmaker* of October 1893, reported the inauguration of classes in bookbinding, on the 16th of the same month, at the Borough Road Polytechnic Institute, (near to the Elephant and Castle in South London, and now the Polytechnic of the South Bank). J. W. Zaehnsdorf was Chairman at this inaugural meeting, and stated that as an employer he had for a long time advocated the need for such classes and had stressed the importance of the public appreciation of bookbinding. He commended the teachers, Mr Parrott for forwarding, and Mr Maullen, whose work as a finisher he had known since completing his own apprenticeship (Fritz Maullen was a beneficiary, in 1886, under the will of Joseph Zaehnsdorf). He hoped that the class would be well filled, and said he would be happy to pay the expenses of his apprentices, and hoped that other employers would do likewise. He also commended *The British Bookmaker* as an excellent trade journal, and spoke of his interest, having conducted it for three years, under its previous title of *The Bookbinder*. In his reply to the vote of thanks, he referred to his book [*The Art of Bookbinding*] and said that he had brought as many copies as his porter could carry; he asked that the institution accept these and give them to the first twenty-six students to be enrolled.

The extensive showroom facilities at the Cambridge Circus premises were required for the substantial bookselling side of the business, and to display the stock of bindings which were available for sale and also served as patterns for customers wishing to commission bindings. For customers unable to visit the showrooms, photographs were sent to them. In photography, J. W. Zaehnsdorf was able to combine business and hobby interests. It is likely that he took the photographs of the new works, used to illustrate *The British Bookmaker* article, and later publicity booklets of the firm. The article in *The British Bookmaker* refers to his skill as an amateur photographer, and his application of this skill to his business needs, by making photographic records of the bindings produced. Regrettably, it would appear that no examples of his photographs of bindings exist today, unless he was responsible for the photographs used to illustrate his book.

The Photographic Club was established in 1879, its first meeting being held on Friday 7 November, at the Freemasons' Tavern, close to the Zaehnsdorf premises in York Street and Catherine Street. Its regular meeting place then became Ashley's Hotel, at 23 Henrietta Street, Covent Garden, still close to the Zaehnsdorf premises. Although J. W. Zaehnsdorf was probably not a founder member, as stated in the obituary by his son, he was certainly an early member of the Club. He had joined by November 1884, and he served on the Committee from 1885 to 1890. In the Annual Reports over this period there are occasional references to his chairing meetings, taking part in discussions, and to his gifts of books to the library, and his free and gratuitous assistance in binding and lettering various volumes. In 1901 he became a Member of the Royal Photographic Society.

J. W. Zaehnsdorf was a member of the volunteer movement, the forerunner of the Territorial Army, and as a young man he served in the London Irish Rifles.* About 1879 he resigned from this Regiment in order to join the Royal Naval Artillery Volunteers. [A copy of the rules of the 1st London Brigade of the Royal Naval Artillery Volunteers, 1874, was presented to the Guildhall Library by his widow in 1931]. In the Naval Artillery Volunteers he reached the rank of leading gunner and rowed stroke in the Captain's gig. He took part in the Naval Review of 1887, held in Hyde Park as part of the Jubilee celebrations for Queen Victoria.

Another hobby interest of J. W. Zaehnsdorf was angling; he was a member of the Piscatorial Society of London, and also its Librarian. Whilst serving as Librarian he produced, in 1902, a typescript catalogue of the library and pictures. A copy of this catalogue is in the British Library [shelf-mark 11913.dd.15], having been presented by his son in February 1933. In addition to the letter from E. Zaehnsdorf, offering this catalogue to the Keeper of Printed Books at the British Museum, there are a few relevant letters to J. W. Zaehnsdorf, and copies of his letters. The Honorary Secretary of the Piscatorial Society, in a letter dated 25 July 1905, sends a copy of a resolution from the half-yearly meeting, expressing the regret the whole of the members of the Society feel at his resignation and recording their cordial appreciation of the excellent work he did for the Society during the many years he held the position of Curator and Librarian. A copy of an earlier letter, dated 13 February 1905, from Zaehnsdorf to his successor as Librarian, offers suggestions and practical advice on discharging the duties. Much later, a letter from Zaehnsdorf, dated 11 January 1916, refers to the premises of the Piscatorial Society, and imparts the information, 'My time in the evening is taken up with night work as a Special Constable . . . so shorthanded is our Division that we are often called out in the middle of the night to go on duty . . .'

More akin to his business interests was J. W. Zaehnsdorf's membership of the Grolier Club of New York. The notice of

* Possibly he joined this regiment because of his Irish ancestry, on his mother's side. Perhaps as immigrants themselves the Zaehnsdorfs felt a sympathy with other immigrants. The maiden names of Joseph Zaehnsdorf's first wife and second one, the mother of J. W. Zaehnsdorf, indicate Irish origins. The names being respectively, Donovan and Mahoney.

his election to membership is dated 3 January 1893, and a letter from the Secretary of the Club, on 12 March 1894, thanks him for 'the gift of the beautiful examples of your work'. The catalogue of an exhibition of mosaic bookbindings, held by The Grolier Club in 1902, includes six bindings attributed to Joseph Zaehnsdorf (1816*–1886).

J. W. Zaehnsdorf was a member of the Committee on Leather for Bookbinding. Towards the end of the nineteenth century it was noticed that the leather bindings in many important libraries were seriously decayed. Acting on a request from the Library Association, the [Royal] Society of Arts assembled a committee of eminent personalities to investigate the causes of this decay, and to suggest remedies. The membership comprised administrators, librarians, leather manufacturers and leather chemists, and five bookbinders: T. J. Cobden-Sanderson, Douglas Cockerell, W. J. Leighton, Miss S. T. Prideaux and J. W. Zaehnsdorf. The committee first met on 3 May 1900, and with admirable promptitude, presented its first report on 17 June 1901. A second, and more detailed, report was published in 1905. The work of this committee was of great importance, as it was the first scientific investigation into the decay of leather bookbindings, and its findings still have validity today.

The activities of the firm were at their zenith in the years after the move to Cambridge Circus. They had held a Special Appointment to H. R. H. the Prince of Wales; and on his accession as King Edward VII the Royal Warrant of Appointment as bookbinders and booksellers was granted to them on 1 November 1901. The appointment to H. R. H. the Prince of Wales followed and, on his accession as King George V, the Royal Appointment was confirmed. Letters from the early years of this century indicate that visits were made to the royal residences to show examples of work.

The years before the First World War saw increasing trade for the firm, as both booksellers and bookbinders, at home and abroad. A series of catalogues were issued over this period (usually undated), and catalogues in French point to the

* This date, as given in the catalogue, should have been 1814.

J. W. Zaehnsdorf and E. J. W. Zaehnsdorf, 1916

European interest. Much of the trade was with America. A collection of Zaehnsdorf bindings was shown at the 1904 World's Fair in St Louis, and was awarded a Grand Prize in the Department of Liberal Arts, British Section, Group 17. In a letter sent in March 1904, informing his American customers of this exhibit, J. W. Zaehnsdorf stated that his son, 'Mr Ernest Zaehnsdorf, who actively assists me in the management of this business, and who has a thorough and practical acquaintance of the art of book-binding, will be in the United States during the months of April, May and June, and will do himself the pleasure of calling upon you.'

With the business now established on a firm basis, and an apparently assured future, it was registered on 30 April 1913 as a private company under the style of Zaehnsdorf Limited, with a capital of £10,000 in one pound shares, to carry on the business of bookbinders, booksellers, stationers, printers, etc. The governing director was J. W. Zaehnsdorf.

The war years of 1914–18 were difficult ones for the newly formed company, as they were for others providing goods, or services, in the nature of luxuries. One former employee, M. O'Brien, in a letter dated 24 January 1915, says that he has accepted a temporary situation due to shortness of work but he will be 'pleased to return when work looks up'. Other letters of the war period, from ex-employees in the army, include those from Driver F. E. Waterhouse; Private W. F. Bowyer, of the City of London Regiment; A. Y. Carter, the London Regiment; Trooper H. Gander, Buckingham Hussars; Rifleman A. V. Sage, Queen Victoria's Rifles; Private W. Adams (apprentice), the Gloucester Regiment. Some correspondents mention members of the family — Charles Buckthorpe, of the Royal Field Artillery refers to 'your son Horace'; J. H. Callaghan thanks Mr Horace for a parcel; and Gunner P. Baucutt of the Royal Field Artillery asks, 'how is Mr Ernest getting on, I suppose he is still drilling recruits?'.

In a later undated letter, Gunner Baucutt, who was based at the Royal Arsenal, Woolwich, passes on what must have been, at that time, highly classified information on ordnance developments. This would have caused great consternation to his superiors had they known it was being sent to someone

Joseph William Zaehnsdorf in the 1920s

with the name Zaehnsdorf. He refers to having 'heard said here that we hope to do better than the Germans by turning out a 20 inch gun during the early part of next spring.' He then writes of 'an aeroplane gun' [presumably an anti-aircraft gun] and a trial firing when it 'blew to atoms and 15 men were killed including an officer.'

No doubt these letters, which have been preserved in a special album, meant much to the family. A copy of a letter, dated 30 November 1918, from J. W. Zaehnsdorf to a Mrs Hallaway, offers sympathy on the death of her son, Fred James, killed in action in the closing days of the war, after being awarded the Military Medal.

The loss of a considerable proportion of his workers, and of two of his sons, to the armed forces must have produced problems for J. W. Zaehnsdorf during the war years, and he had to appeal to the authorities for the deferment, or exemption, from call-up of his men. Two letters indicate the effects military service was having on his workshops. On 21 November 1916 he wrote to the Chief Recruiting Officer requesting a further extension from call-up of one of his men. He stated that about three-quarters of the staff had joined the forces and this was having considerable effect. They had a large number of export orders which must be shipped before Christmas, and also Christmas work for the King and the Queen. An important part of this work was executed by the man on whose behalf he was writing, a foreman and cutter out named Walker, and no men of military age were left in the workshops. He referred to his three sons, two of whom were in the Army, and the other who had been too ill to work for a considerable time. On 3 June 1918 he wrote to the Lambeth Tribunal requesting the exemption of Arthur Herbert Molyneux, who had been in his employ for 33 years. He said that his usual staff numbered from 90 to 100, but the majority had been called up and he was left with 16 all told.

In pre-war days possession of a Germanic name was probably of some advantage to a bookbinder, following the great tradition of immigrant German binders to England. However, during the war this was far from the case, when latent xenophobia and misguided patriotism directed much abuse against anyone suspected of having German antecedents. So families such as the Battenbergs, and even the Royal Family, decided to change their names. An early indication of problems for the company is given by a letter dated 2 October 1914, with a footnote asking, 'whether the Directors and chief shareholders of "Zaehnsdorf" are British subjects'.* Members of the family served their country in the war; J. W. Zaehnsdorf's service in the Special Constabulary has already been noted, and two of his sons served in the army — Ernest in the Artists' Rifles, as a Sergeant Instructor at the School of Musketry, Hythe, later to be commissioned in the Royal Marines; and his brother Horace served in the Royal Fusiliers. After nearly four years of war, these two sons both changed their names whilst in the army. The eldest, Ernest Joseph Watts Zaehnsdorf, changed his name by the simple expedient of abandoning the name Zaehnsdorf. This was effected by a deed poll dated 27 May 1918 and announced in *The London Gazette* of 4 June 1918 when his home address is given as Watford. However, in spite of this he continued, throughout his life, to use the name Zaehnsdorf for all business purposes. His brother, Horace Edwin, also changed his name to Watts, and took the name Horace Edwin Watts, by a deed poll dated 10 June 1918 and announced in *The London Gazette* of 26 July 1918, when he is described as 'Bookbinder, now a Private in the Royal Fusiliers', and gives his parents' address, 13 Tavistock Square, London. Although the two brothers changed their name, their parents and brother, Arthur Gerald, retained their surname of Zaehnsdorf until their deaths, and their sister, Dora, only changed her name to Cotton on her marriage.

A more light-hearted aspect of the name of the family and company is the number of mis-spellings which have been perpetrated. A file of these exists labelled, 'How not to spell Zaehnsdorf', and contains many examples. One of the more

* Possibly as a result of this, correspondence from the firm during the war years, 1914–1918, carried a label, size 4 × 2½ inches, printed in red, and giving the information — 'The Directors, Staff and Workmen of Messrs. ZAEHNSDORF, LTD., are British Subjects. The business was established in London, 1842, *Vide* — Dictionary of National Biography. The Firm has no connection with Germany nor with German Capital'.

surprising is an impression of a block, some 10 × 9 cm, with the lettering, 'ZAEHSDORF's Revolving Book Case'. A note adds the information that 'the tool cutter had worked for the house 12 years and it was blocked by a workman who has been here for 27 years'. Other examples from various items of correspondence show almost every conceivable mis-spelling of the name. Officialdom had much difficulty but probably excelled itself with the entry in the Index of Births for September 1881, where a son of J. W. Zaehnsdorf, Arthur Gerald, (the one who was to retain the name), is given two separate adjoining entries, under 'ZAETENSDORF' and 'ZAETINSDORF'.

After the war, Joseph William Zaehnsdorf continued his active and controlling position in the business only until 1920, when he retired and handed over to his son, Ernest Joseph Watts Zaehnsdorf. In his retirement he retained an interest in the business, and he also played an active part in many movements in the town of Deal, where he resided. His interests included the British Legion and the collection of goods and funds to provide Christmas cheer for the men serving on the lightships. He died, at Deal, of a sudden heart attack, on 21 October 1930, aged 77 years. At his funeral a guard of honour was provided by the British Legion, and the esteem of the townsfolk of Deal was indicated by the flying of flags at half-mast. In addition to the family mourners, the staff of Zaehnsdorf Limited were represented at the funeral by Mr George Page, the oldest employee, who had been with the company for over 40 years, and Mr Sydney Jones, the Secretary of the Shop Association. The death of J. W. Zaehnsdorf was widely reported in the trade press, local newspapers, and, in addition, obituaries appeared in *The Anglers' News* of 25 October 1930, and in *The Field* of 8 November 1930.

Ernest Joseph Watts Zaehnsdorf, 1921

3

Ernest Zaehnsdorf
1879–1970

Ernest Joseph Watts Zaehnsdorf was the eldest son of Joseph William, and grandson of Joseph Zaehnsdorf, the founder of the firm. He was born in 1879, and entered the firm in 1896, succeeding his father in 1920. As had both his grandfather and father, he too, had received a thorough training as a practical bookbinder. Like his father he was active in promulgating the principles of sound bookbinding. His first lecture on bookbinding, which was illustrated by practical demonstrations and an exhibition of bindings, was delivered at Stationers' Hall on Friday 9 February 1923, under the auspices of the Stationers' Company and Printing Industry Technical Board.

During the course of his wide-ranging survey, Ernest Zaehnsdorf referred to the antiquity of bookbinding, and pointed out that, whilst the craft of bookbinding long predates that of printing, there had been few changes in the actual methods of bookbinding. He discussed paper cleaning by dry and wet methods, and mentioned foxing. He showed examples of ordinary commercial 'sawn-in' sewing and contrasted it with flexible sewing on bands or cords, which he recommended for hard wear; he also described other types of sewing, including French, overcasting, and machine sewing. He said that end papers should be chosen to be in keeping with the book. The processes of bookbinding were described, in turn, to the final process of finishing, when he made a plea for legible lettering. Discussing the design of book covers he referred to inlaid work, of which many examples of Zaehnsdorf work were available for inspection, and in his concluding comment suggested that bookbinders, in respect of design, were in danger of getting into a rut. In addition to the lecture there was a demonstration of the processes of bookbinding and many exhibits of Zaehnsdorf bindings.

The Worshipful Company of Stationers

A series of technical lectures arranged by the Stationers' Company and
Printing Industry Technical Board

An Address on

Bookbinding

will be given by

E. J. W. ZAEHNSDORF, Esq.

(ZAEHNSDORF, LIMITED)

AT STATIONERS' HALL
Ludgate Hill, London, E.C.4
at 6.30 p.m. on

Friday, 9th Feb., 1923

Synopsis :

Antiquity of Craft—Paper suitable for Binding—Folding
(signatures)—Collating : (a) old books, (b) cleaning—Sewing :
ordinary, flexible, tapes, French, machine—End Papers—
Rounding—Backing—Lacing in—Edge Gilding—Headbanding—Lining up—Covering—Siding—Pasting Down—Finish-
ing : lettering, panelling, tooling generally, inlaying in colour.

Chairman :

MAJOR R. LEIGHTON
Chairman Bookbinding Section, London Chamber of Commerce

Time Allowed for Questions and Discussion.

THE ADDRESS WILL BE ILLUSTRATED BY PRACTICAL
DEMONSTRATIONS AND AN EXHIBITION OF BINDINGS.

THE LECTURES ARE OPEN TO ALL INTERESTED.

In opening the question and discussion period, the Honorary Secretary of the Technical Board, Mr J. R. Riddell, congratulated Ernest Zaehnsdorf on his first public lecture. The next day he wrote to thank him 'for the interesting and informative Lecture', stating that 'it has been commented upon that it is difficult to understand how you could have achieved so great a success in giving for the first time, your encyclopedic address which gained the admiration of the whole of your audience.' The writer also requested that thanks to be conveyed to 'Mr Harrison* and his colleagues, . . . for all they did to make the meeting last night an outstanding one in the series of Technical Lectures which has been held at Stationers' Hall during this session'. He ended by mentioning his own pride in finding such a technical lecturer, and suggested that many requests would follow for future lectures. Perhaps the Honorary Secretary of the Technical Board was aware of forthcoming events, or was able to shape them, but this prediction was shortly to be fulfilled in a most remarkable fashion. In only a few weeks time Ernest Zaehnsdorf was to give, whilst public broadcasting was in its infancy, what was undoubtedly the first radio talk on bookbinding.

This talk, of some eight minutes duration, was delivered on the evening of Saturday 12 May 1923, following the news bulletin and weather forecast, and was from the London Broadcasting Station of the British Broadcasting Company, which had only commenced daily broadcasting six months

---

* Thomas Harrison (1876–1955). the son of a Westmorland stone mason, was apprenticed as a finisher to Fazakerley's the Liverpool bookbinders. After his apprenticeship he undertook a course on art and design at the Liverpool College of Art. He went to London as a journeyman finisher and worked in several West End shops, including Zaehnsdorfs, where he became manager. He moved to H. T. Wood, where he became the proprietor but the slump of the early 1930s resulted in the firm going into liquidation. About 1934 he became technical adviser to Nevett Ltd, of Colindale, and from 1939 until his death, in 1955, he was self-employed. He taught at the Northampton Polytechnic, the London School of Printing, and during the war years at the Sutton School of Art. He was appointed a Member of the British Empire, for services to bookbinding, in the New Year's Honours List of 1946. His, *The Bookbinding Craft and Industry*, was first published in 1926. The Thomas Harrison Memorial Fund was inaugurated in November 1955, on the initiative of H. A. de Coverly, in the form of an annual award for craft bookbinding, to be competed for by student craftsmen.

47

Opposite: Announcement of Address on Bookbinding

D

earlier, on 14 November 1922. It was a masterpiece of compression, including in its purview, an introductory history of records and early bookbinding, the enemies of books, books bound in human skin — a topic of never-failing macabre fascination, the binding of miniature books, and fore-edge painting. This talk still has interest — as the first broadcast on bookbinding and also because of its subject matter; its full text is given in Appendix C.

The company, and its principals, were obviously willing to utilize and exploit the then developing methods of mass communication, for the general benefit of the craft of bookbinding, and the education of the public and the information of those likely to commission work. During November 1933, a short film, to be entitled *Turning Over An Old Leaf*, was shot at the Cambridge Works. This showed, in a series of ten shots, the various processes in re-binding an old book. It started with a view of the dilapidated condition of the book, then showed sewing on leather thongs, shaping the book to give the rounded spine and backing to form the shoulders in which the boards fit. The attachment of wooden boards by hammering wooden dowels into holes in the boards to fasten the thongs was shown, followed by a close-up view of the boards in position with the projecting dowels ready to be trimmed flush. Paring of a piece of pigskin was shown, and then covering the book with the pigskin, followed by tying of temporary cords, around the raised bands on the spine, which remain in position until the paste adhesive for the leather covering had dried. The closing shot showed brush and ink lettering of the book. The final edited film was of approximately three minutes duration, and was used with two other short films, to form an issue of the Gaumont-British *Cinemagazine*, which was shown at cinemas in February 1934.*

For the first volume of the *American Book Collector*, published in 1932, Ernest Zaehnsdorf contributed two articles. The first issue, in January 1932, contained a paper on 'The Preservation of Leather Bindings', of which he was joint

---

* A description of the film, with eight small stills, was given in *The British and Colonial Printer and Stationer* of 15 February 1934.

author together with C. I. Hutchins, late Keeper of the Gennadius Collection. This discussed the efficacy, or lack of it, of leather dressings for the preservation of bookbindings, and warned strongly against the use of waxes. A composition was advocated which had been available for five or six years and whose preparation was stated to be 'beyond the facilities of the amateur, but the Editor will be pleased to supply further details to anyone interested'. The second article in the sixth (June) issue had Ernest Zaehnsdorf as sole author and was on 'Preservation by Repair' and touched on the scientific aspects of book conservation. Acknowledgement was made to Mr C. M. Bernard, Staff Research Chemist of Messrs Zaehnsdorf Limited, for technical assistance with details concerning the chemical aspects of the treatment of paper. This early employment of a research chemist indicates the prudent attitude of the company to the preservation of books and documents entrusted to their care.

During the autumn of 1935, Ernest Zaehnsdorf addressed the London Associates of the Associated Booksellers of Great Britain and Ireland on 'Orders to the Bookbinder', when he discussed the nature of instructions to the bookbinder and some points to be remembered when specifying bookbinding requirements. This talk gave much useful advice, based on many years of practical experience, and was reminiscent of the talk which his father gave to the Library Association in 1886. After a lapse of almost fifty years, the audience was again told of the importance of the choice of materials, and of sound sewing. The treatment of book edges, choice of endpapers, and decorative finishing were all mentioned, along with the necessity for customers to use technical terms with great care, and correctly!

Shortly after the above talk, Thomas Harrison, who had then left the employ of Zaehnsdorf's, spoke to the December 1935 meeting of the Printing, Bookbinding and Kindred Trades' Overseers Association on 'A Retrospect of Fifty Years of Bookbinding'. He gave a fairly detailed account of the time which he had spent at Zaehnsdorf's, and discussed the nature of his work there, and commented on the old classic French styles of binding for which they were so well known.

His own success was as a result of gaining, whilst employed there, the only full technological certificate in bookbinding to be awarded for many years.

By the time that Ernest Zaehnsdorf took over direction of the firm its expansionist days were over. The aftermath of the First World War and resulting political and social changes throughout Europe affected their traditional clientele, as did the trade and economic depression of the 1920s and early 1930s which had serious consequences in the United States of America. The problems of this period were responsible for the demise of some well-known firms of craft binders, including de Coverly, Fazakerley, Ramage, and Riviere. There is evidence of attempts to stimulate interest and sales, from a finely printed invitation, of 1931, for a private exhibition of rare books and fine bindings, sponsored jointly by The Grolier Book Shop of London, New York, and Kansas City, and by Zaehnsdorf Limited. In 1932 Ernest Zaehnsdorf had to apply for, and was granted by the lessors, a reduction in the rent of the Cambridge Works. In his request he referred to the unsatisfactory trading results of the last two years, and added that a slight improvement in home trade, and with some return of the American trade, gave hope that they could pull through. A year later he requested that the rent concession be granted again as there had been no improvement in trade. Serious consideration was also given at this time to sub-letting the ground floor showroom and the basement. Any expectations arising from the general improvement in the economic climate of the late 1930s were soon to be dashed, in 1939, by the outbreak of the Second World War.

At the time that the war ended in 1945, Ernest Zaehnsdorf was near the normal retiring age. This, together with the fact that the post-war years heralded a period of economic gloom for the United Kingdom, were most likely important causative factors in the company passing from the control of the Zaehnsdorf family. The owners of the company had been exclusively members of the family until 1936, when, for the first time, names other than Zaehnsdorf appear as members. Ernest Zaehnsdorf was the majority shareholder until March 1947, when he disposed of the bulk of his holding. On

10 December 1947 the share capital was divided into 100,000 shares of two shillings (10p) each, and a list of shareholders of that date shows Ernest Zaehnsdorf holding 10 shares, as did two other members, the remaining 99,970 shares being held by Cecil Adrian Hatry, a director of T. Werner Laurie Ltd. On 5 November 1948, Mr Hatry retired from the board of Zaehnsdorf Limited, and was replaced by Colonel Hubert Bruce Logan, whose other directorships included Hatchards Ltd. Following the 1950 Annual General Meeting, the list of members of the company shows Hatchards Ltd owning 99,990 of the shares, with the remaining 10 being held by William Dennis Dereham. In 1952, Hatchards issued a booklet, *Notes on the Art of Bookbinding*, and, in addition to their name, the front cover also carried, 'and its Associated Bindery Zaehnsdorf Ltd'.

A Special Resolution of Zaehnsdorf Limited was passed on 26 March 1957, that the name of the company be changed to 'Book Trading Company Limited'. At an Extraordinary Meeting of Hartram Limited on 8 May 1957, a Special Resolution was passed that the name be changed to Zaehnsdorf Limited, and this resulted in the re-emergence of the company under its present owners. However, these events carry the Zaehnsdorf story beyond the period when the company was under the control of members of the family; an era which ended in March 1947 — more than one hundred years after the young immigrant bookbinder, Joseph Zaehnsdorf, made the first attempts at founding his business in London.

Ernest Joseph Watts Zaehnsdorf continued as a director of the company until March 1957. He moved from Watford to Hastings in 1947, and died there on 20 April 1970, at the age of ninety years.

An early Zaehnsdorf Binding (203 × 140mm)
(Courtesy British Library)

4

Some Zaehnsdorf Bindings

The firm of Zaehnsdorf established an enviable reputation for the production of the finest bindings. Whilst the charge probably could be upheld that their designs tended to be imitative, following the examples of the past, rather than innovative, it is possible that this was necessary to meet the demands from customers. In 1874 Joseph Zaehnsdorf advertised 'Bookbinding in the monastic, Grolier, Maioli and Illuminated Styles'. The workmanship and execution of their bindings were of the highest order and they produced bindings for the great collectors in England, America, Europe, and other parts of the world. As a result examples of Zaehnsdorf bindings are to be found today in most of the great collections, either still remaining in private hands, or, more usually, in public collections in libraries and museums; and many are illustrated in standard works on bookbinding. This is particularly true of bindings emanating from the heyday of the firm, the period corresponding approximately from after the move to Cambridge Circus in 1890, to the outbreak of the World War in 1914. Fewer examples are to be found of the early work of the firm, when Joseph Zaehnsdorf was establishing his business. The vast number of Zaehnsdorf bindings precludes any attempt at a comprehensive survey within the present limits. Instead, it is hoped that a description of a few selected items, some slightly unusual, or of special interest, will give an indication of the nature and scope of the firm's activities.

An Early Zaehnsdorf Binding

The earliest known example of a Zaehnsdorf binding has been mentioned in connection with the first business address of Joseph Zaehnsdorf. This is a 'cathedral' binding in black calf, blocked in blind with a large plaque of the west front of York

Minster, on an 1836 edition of Luther's Version of the Bible, in German. Whilst this is in no way a great binding, but typical of the embossed bindings of the period, its age, in relation to the business, gives it added importance for the present study, and it has other intriguing aspects that claim further consideration. It was formerly in the collection of J. W. Hely-Hutchinson and sold by Sotheby's on 12 March 1956, as lot 91. It is illustrated in the sale catalogue where it is stated to have been bound about 1845, and wrongly described as being in blue cloth (it is bound in black calf, and its fitted box is of blue cloth). This binding was sold with a letter from Ernest Zaehnsdorf, dated 14 October 1946, giving the information that it is the earliest binding by the firm known to him, and the only example of this ticket which he had met. He also gave the information that the patterned roll, used to decorate the turn-in of the book, was still in their possession [Zaehnsdorf Limited still have the roll] and as signature to the letter he used an impression of this roll.

This volume most likely passed into the possession of Ernest Zaehnsdorf early in 1944, from Arthur Rogers, a bookseller of Newcastle-upon-Tyne, who wrote to Zaehnsdorfs on 29 December 1943, indicating that he had this book, enclosing a rubbing of the binding and asking whether Zaehnsdorfs had 'actually executed the binding or merely sold it'. The following day Ernest Zaehnsdorf replied that his interest was excited as he had 'never seen one of our original binding labels of so early a date'. He continued — 'I consider that the possibility that the label was inserted in a book sold —as a bookseller might do — may be ruled out. It is far more likely to be a genuine binders label. The block is not in our possession to-day as possibly it may have been discarded in 1889 when we moved here from Catherine St, Strand. A number of tools and blocks were so discarded as "old fashioned" and unlikely to be used again'. The next day Ernest Zaehnsdorf again wrote to Arthur Rogers, referring to his letter of the previous day and asking if he might have sight of the binding, offering to return it speedily and pay carriage both ways. Whilst no further correspondence is preserved on this matter, it would appear that Ernest Zaehnsdorf must have purchased the book from Arthur Rogers, and then, at some later date, before October 1946, re-sold it to J. W. Hely-Hutchinson. It was bought at the Hely-Hutchinson sale on behalf of Henry Davis, and the volume is now in the British Library; it was described and illustrated by Mirjam M. Foot, in *The Henry Davis Gift*, Vol. II, (1983), entry No 218.

Another cathedral binding in the British Library is on T. H. Horne's, *Landscape Illustration of The Bible*, Vol. II, 1836. This binding, by Westley, is also embossed with an elevation of the west front of York Minster, and is described and illustrated (as entry 26) by Eleanore Jamieson in her *English Embossed Bindings 1825–1850*, (Cambridge, 1972). Inspection of this volume and the one discussed previously, indicates that they were both embossed from the same die, which is signed in both cases, as may be seen, using a lens, from the illustrations in Mrs Jamieson's book and the Sotheby Catalogue; up the lower left-hand corner 'WESTLEY' and up the lower right-hand corner 'LONDON'. This raises doubts as to whether or not Zaehnsdorf did actually bind the volume containing his ticket, although the decoration on the turn-in, made by a roll still in the possession of the firm, tends to confirm that he did. At least this binding, if Zaehnsdorf had access to, or later possessed, the Westley die, provides evidence of a connection between Zaehnsdorf and Westley, by whom he was employed when he first came to England.

A further use, of what is obviously the same die, is present on a royal 8vo copy of the Book of Common Prayer, published in 1844, and used to illustrate an article on stock or publishers' bindings in *The British and Colonial Printer and Stationer*, of 18 April 1907. Whilst showing a further use of the die, it, unfortunately, does not help the present enquiry, since no further details are given of the binding, other than that the design has some pretensions to accuracy of detail.

In one of his letters to Arthur Rogers, Ernest Zaehnsdorf mentioned that an intention of his, of compiling a history of the firm, had been defeated by his father disposing of all the original books of accounts during the First World War. It is a pity that during his long life Ernest Zaehnsdorf never produced such a history, thus depriving us of much information

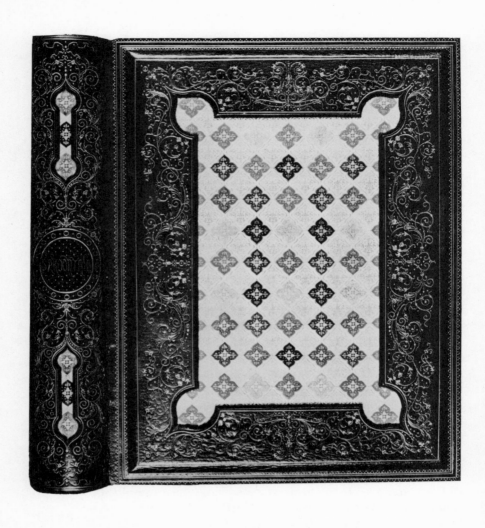

Binding of *Sakoontala* (233 × 170mm)
(Courtesy British Library)

on the firm and its bindings. Happily all is not entirely lost, because the diligent searcher can find useful snippets in the accounts of the various talks which Ernest Zaehnsdorf gave, and in his short contributions to the trade and other periodicals of the 1930s. Three further Zaehnsdorf bindings in the British Library, in addition to being superb examples of the bookbinders' craft, have some information about them which he contributed, and which adds interest to the Zaehnsdorf story. Two of these bindings were donated by him to the British Museum, as an act of public spiritedness and of family piety, as examples of the work of his grandfather and father.

A Binding for the International Exhibition, 1862

In 1855 Stephen Austin, the Oriental printer of Hertford, published a translation by Professor Monier-William of Haileybury College, of a Sanskrit drama — *Sakoontala*, by the Indian poet and dramatist Kalidasa, who lived about the third century A.D. This was an outstanding example of mid-nineteenth century book production — the decorations by T. Sulman, junior, were copied from manuscripts in the British Museum, and engraved by George Meason. The borders surrounding the text were printed in four colours. The publisher's binding* of the leather-bound edition was an elaborate Oriental design, blocked in gold, and the edges of the book were gauffered. This book created considerable interest when it was published and Stephen Austin received several awards for his work. Joseph Zaehnsdorf, no doubt responding to this interest, bound copies of the book and one of these was presented to the British Museum, now the British Library [press-mark C.68.i.15] by his grandson in January 1932. This is a beautiful binding, and a fine example of techniques, in sympathy with both the subject matter of the book and its sumptuous style of production.

This binding is in brown morocco, elaborately gold-tooled with a fine arabesque pattern, each board having a large central sunk panel of white leather, inlaid with coloured and

---

* Described by James Moran in his, *Stephen Austin's of Hertford*, (1968), page 32.

Binding of *Mireille* (437 × 300mm)
(Courtesy British Library)

gilt arabesque patterns of red, blue, green and citron. The spine is decorated with fine arabesque gold-tooling, the title is on a central green panel, and there are two small sunken panels of decorated white leather. The turn-in on the doublures is gold-tooled with red, blue and green inlays, and the centre panel is white with red, blue and green inlays in outline. The bottom centre of the white panel on the front doublure is signed 'BOUND BY ZAEHNSDORF'. The fly-leaves are dark brown watered-silk and the edges of the book are gilded and gauffered. The size of the volume is 233 × 170 mm, and it is enclosed in a cask-like box, fitted with a lock, and lined with padded green watered-silk.

Ernest Zaehnsdorf's presentation inscription states that the binding is the work of Joseph Zaehnsdorf (1814–1886) and was designed and executed by him about 1856. A subsequent letter from him, dated 7 May 1935, states that as a result of looking through some notes on bookbindings he had found a record that *Sakoontala* was exhibited at the Exhibition of 1862. The *Bookbinders' Trade Circular* of 12 August 1862, in a review of the bookbinding entries at the exhibition, describes a folio edition of Dante's *L'Inferno*, decorated in elaborate scroll-work with the inside of the cover also elaborately finished, and shown by reflection in a piece of looking-glass placed under the book, and in addition accompanied by photographs of the inner and outer cover decoration. Mention was also made of a small quarto 'with a sunk centre in illuminated work most elaborately finished, which many would prefer to the folio'. This reference is undoubtedly to the *Sakoontala*. Other examples of Zaehnsdorf bindings were also mentioned in the review, including two 32mo volumes in red morocco.

Louis Genth

One of the Zaehnsdorf bindings in the British Library [press-mark C.68.k.2] has added interest because its finishing may be attributed, with reasonable certainty, to a particular workman. This is on a copy of *Mireille* (Paris, 1884) by the Provençal poet, Frédéric Mistral, and is Copy No 48 of an edition of 150 copies on Japanese vellum, 'papier japon'. It is a folio volume, size 437 ×300 mm, bound in orange morocco; the covers have a pattern of acanthus leaves inlaid in green and tooled in gold, and the doublures are tooled. The second panel from the bottom is not decorated or lettered as are the others. The paper pattern used for the inlaid and tooled pattern of the covers is pasted on one of the rear end-leaves.

This binding was the subject of a short note by Ernest Zaehnsdorf in *The British and Colonial Printer and Stationer*, of 21 January 1932. It had been presented to the British Museum by a Mr Julian Moore, and the Museum authorities had sought some information about the book. As a result of enquiries at Zaehnsdorf's, Mr George Page, who had joined the firm in 1888, was positive that the tooling was the work of a finisher employed by Joseph Zaehnsdorf, a Frenchman and fine craftsman named Louis Genth [Ernest Zaehnsdorf confused the binder's name with that of the Belgian City, describing him as, Ghent]. Genth lived and worked in London for many years, and was employed by Joseph Zaehnsdorf from 1859 to 1886. Since this edition of *Mireille* was not published until 1884, it must have been among some of the last work which he did for the elder Zaehnsdorf, who died in 1886, possibly being carried out whilst the firm was under the active management of J. W. Zaehnsdorf. Ernest Zaehnsdorf reprints an entry from a private notebook, kept by his grandfather, concerning employees [now in the possession of Mr B. C. Middleton, and the property of the Rochester Institute of Technology. New York]. The entry referring to Louis Genth, made at the time of the 1872 strike, is as follows,

Mr Louis Genth, extra finisher 28/9/72
Left on Strike in consequence of employing Non Society Men and foreigners, he is himself a foreigner, has been thirteen years with me. First Class extra finisher and particularly in Inlaying, very industrious when he likes and also very lazy at other times, not over honestly.

His weekly wage was stated as forty-eight shillings (£2.40). An entry by Ernest Zaehnsdorf in this notebook, added opposite Joseph's entry for Genth, and dated 18 January 1932, quotes from a letter, which he had received that day, from his mother, giving the information that she remembers Genth as 'a typical dark Frenchman rather small and very vivacious'.

Louis Genth was undoubtedly a fine craftsman, especially since Joseph Zaehnsdorf re-employed him after the 1872 strike, and appears to have been something of a complex personality. Ernest Zaehnsdorf in his note on the *Mireille* binding draws largely on supposition to contrast the characters of his grandfather and his employee, when he states, 'Here we have a remarkable contrast of racial characteristics. The employer, a man of Teuton upbringing, to whom every day is a working day, full of energy and without respite. The Frenchman, imbued with a temperamental character of an artistic type, working almost feverishly on a book when the spirit moves him and producing a fine result; but when the work is finished, he feels tired and perhaps his thoughts are with congenial companions in a café — certainly not in the bookbinding workshop. His employer cannot understand these moods. . . . because he cannot appreciate the Gallic view'.

Genth's fine workmanship, affirmed by his employer, also received other contemporary acknowledgement, when he gained one of the prizes for art-workmen offered in 1864 by the Society of Arts. These prizes were first announced in 1863, and were for ten different manufacturing processes, but did not include bookbinding. Details of the first awards, for 1864, were given in the *Journal of the Society of Arts*, for 11 March 1864, and the number of classes had been increased to 18. One of these, 17(a), was for bookbinding, with a prize of £7. 10s. (£7.50) for the best and a second prize of £5 for the next best work executed after an Italian specimen in the South Kensington Museum, No. 7,925. The book to be bound being specified as some classical author of the size given. Photographs of the specimen being available for one shilling (5p). The Society's *Journal* for 6 January 1865 listed the entries for the various classes, and showed a single entry for bookbinding after an Italian specimen by Louis Genth, 15 Broad Court, Bow Street, London W.C., with the binder's price for the work being £8. 8s. (£8.40). Three weeks later the prize winners were announced and Genth received the first prize

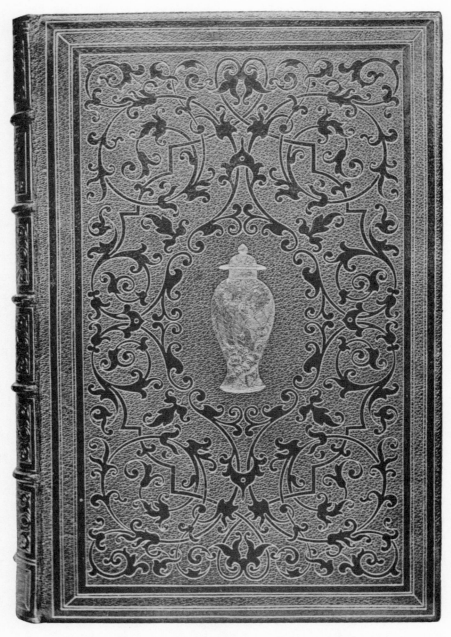

Binding of *Histoire Artistique de la Porcelaine* (c. 340 × 225mm)
(from *The British Bookbinder*, July 1890)

for his entry which, although the only one in its class, the adjudicators thought sufficiently highly of to make the award. The book was described as being bound for the South Kensington Museum from the pattern and was 'partly in the Grolier and partly in the Maioli styles, illuminated in black and white colours'. The *Bookbinders' Trade Circular*, of 28 March 1865, in reporting this award, referred to it being made to a member of our society, Mr. L. Genth, and mentioned that specimens of his workmanship were exhibited in the Great Exhibition of 1861 [presumably 1862?]. It is possible, therefore, that his skill, 'particularly in inlaying', as mentioned by Joseph Zaehnsdorf in his report book, may have contributed to the *Sakoontala* and other bindings exhibited by Zaehnsdorf in the 1862 Exhibition. It is, therefore, a matter for reasonable speculation as to how much the skill of Genth contributed to the establishment of Joseph Zaehnsdorf's business, since he joined the firm in 1859, and Zaehnsdorf's first public recognition was the Honourable mention which he received at the 1862 Exhibition.

In 1866 Genth entered a further binding in the Competition for Art Workmanship which was described as being in the 'early Florentine style'. This was on a copy of *Histoire de la Porcelaine*. For this binding Genth had placed a price of £35 (a fairly considerable sum for those days, representing over three month's wages for him). He also entered two other bindings, for which no details were given other than their prices of £8. 8s. and £10. 10s. (£8.40 and £10.50). On 1 February 1867, the Society's *Journal* announced that he had been awarded a prize of £5. On this occasion Genth's address was given as 30 Brydges Street, Covent Garden, W.C., which was the address of Zaehnsdorf's bindery at that time. Whilst this binding of Genth's has not been located, it is possible that it is illustrated, as an example of the Florentine style, in J. W. Zaehnsdorf's *The Art of Bookbinding*. A plate of this binding was published as a supplement to *The British Bookmaker*, July 1890, when the binding is described as: '*Histoire Artistique de la Porcelaine*, Jacquemart (Paris, 1862), a small folio bound in brown levant morocco, super extra, elaborately inlaid with red morocco to a Florentine pattern'. The date of this book

E

could fit with it having been bound for 1866, and the elaborately inlaid style of binding is one in which Genth apparently excelled. The block, of an Eastern vase, used as the centre-piece of this binding is still in the possession of the company.

Centre-piece for *Histoire Artistique de
la Porcelaine* (full size)

Catalogue No. 1: French, issued by J. Zaehnsdorf from 14 York Street, in 1887, lists copies of both *Mireille* and Jacquemart's *Histoire Artistique de la Porcelaine*, which were priced at £50 and £80 respectively. The descriptions, given in this catalogue, of the bindings of these volumes are not sufficiently detailed to make it possible to state without doubt that they are the bindings referred to above. Also it is possible that Zaehnsdorf bound more than one copy of these works. Nevertheless, the descriptions given are not at variance with those of Genth's bindings, and the editions are the correct ones, so it is possible that these were his work.

On 14 February 1868 the *Journal of the Society of Arts*, giving the prize winners for the entries submitted in the previous year, referred to a binding by Genth on *De Imitatione Christi*, which was 'Highly commended, but ineligible for a prize having received an award in the same item in a former competition'. Without this rule there was a chance that Genth might have made this prize his monopoly.

There is further notice of Louis Genth about this time, and again in connection with the Society of Arts. He was one of the artisans selected to visit the Paris Universal Exhibition of 1867, under a scheme organised by the Society. This is perhaps not surprising since his work was known to the Society by his success in the Art Workmanship Competition, and the fact that French was his native language would have been an advantage. A list of contributors to the fund for sending these workmen to Paris included his employer, Joseph Zaehnsdorf, as a contributor of half-a-guinea (52.5p).

In accordance with the regulations for the scheme for assisting these artisans to visit the exhibition, Louis Genth submitted a report to the Society which was published in the printed volume of reports.* This is one of the shorter reports and expressed his regret that he had been unable to accomplish the main object of his visit. The cases of the books on exhibition were all closed with no one present to open them, to enable him to judge the real merits of the bindings. Further, he had been unable to obtain access to any workshops where extra binding was undertaken, and so was not able to report on the way in which the various workshops were conducted. It is perhaps surprising that Genth, as a Frenchman, could not gain access to these binderies and would appear to indicate a degree of suspicion, or lack of cordiality, between the binders of the two nations. A similar situation, but in the reverse direction, existed some twenty-five years later, and was reported in *The British Bookmaker*, of December 1892, when a French binder, sent to London by the Chambre Syndicale of the binding trade in Paris, was refused admission to the Zaehnsdorf bindery.

---

* *Reports of Artisans: Paris Universal Exhibition 1867*. London: Published for the Society of Arts by Bell & Daldy, 1867.

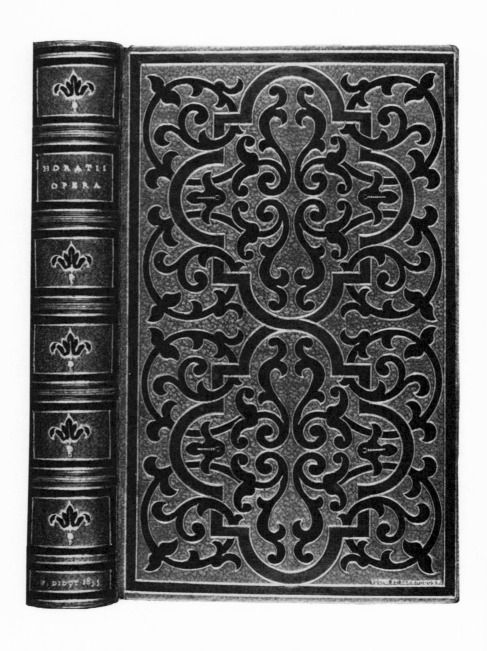

Binding of Quinti Horatii Flacci, *Opera* (141 × 84mm)
(Courtesy British Library)

Referring to the display of bookbindings at the exhibition, Genth commented on the small number of firms represented, both from France and England, the only London binders being Zaehnsdorf, Ramage and Hammond, with Ward and Co., of Belfast. He adjudged the work exhibited to be as fine a collection of binding as produced in the nineteenth century, and, therefore, it was no surprise that the majority of medals for binding were awarded to the English. He was critical of the French finishing. Concluding his report, Genth commented on the general behaviour in public, civility, sobriety and intelligence of the French journeyman bookbinders, which he considered to be in advance of English working men. He made a plea for the liberalization of Sunday observance in England, to enable English workers to enjoy some of the privileges available to their neighbours. He also remarked that the cleanliness of the streets and open spaces of Paris was far in advance of that of London.

A Binding by J. W. Zaehnsdorf

To return, after the digression to consider the work of Louis Genth, to the three Zaehnsdorf bindings in the British Library for which there is some background information, somewhat less is known about the third of these. This is a binding by Joseph William Zaehnsdorf, and the inscription by his son, on one of the end-papers, summarises its story,

Presented to The British Museum in
memory of
Joseph William Zaehnsdorf
(1853–1930)
who bound this book for the
Paris Exhibition
1889
E. Zaehnsdorf
June 1932

The binding is on a copy of Quinti Horatii Flacci, *Opera* (Paris 1855) [press-mark C.72.a.12]. It is of orange morocco with an interlacing strapwork design inlaid in black and red. The doublures are of dark brown morocco with a border, tooled with a finely-cut roll. The binding is signed in the continental fashion on the bottom right hand corner of the upper cover: BOUND BY ZAEHNSDORF.

Designer Bindings

The three Zaehnsdorf bindings discussed previously, whilst demonstrating workmanship of the highest standard, rely for their desigms on stylized patterns of the past, as did the other binders of the period. In Joseph Zaehnsdorf's advertisement in the Catalogue of the 1874 London International Exhibition, he offered bookbindings in the monastic, Grolier, Maioli and illuminated styles, and it was for these styles, rather than fashion, by which Zaehnsdorf bindings were recognised. It may, therefore, have been an attempt to break with the past that resulted in Zaehnsdorfs entering some bindings designed by Lewis Foreman Day (1845–1910) in the fourth, 1893, show of The Arts and Crafts Exhibition Society. Day was a prominent decorative artist of the period, and a designer of textiles, tiles and glass, and a Master of the Art Workers' Guild. The bookbinding exhibits, particularly the work of amateurs, were obviously not to the taste of the reviewer of the show in *The British Bookmaker*, of November 1893, who refers to 'the exhibition of some of the worst trash in bookbinding which it has ever been our lot to view. . . . These wretched objects are exhibited side by side with the tooling of Mr F. Maullen, of Zaehnsdorf's, and of course they suffer by the comparison'. The firm had entered four volumes of poetry, a two-volume Herrick, and a volume each of Wyatt and Surrey, all being designed by Lewis F. Day and tooled by F. Maullen. The article contains illustrations* of the bindings of each of the three authors' works. The reviewer admits the designs to be 'perhaps a stage above mediocrity', and criticizes the design of the leaf work, and the use of a single dot tool instead of dotted gouges for tooling the design, claiming that 'Lewis Day wants to better nature and the Creator's design in his own; and beside, instead of adopting the technique of the craft in the

---

* These three bindings were also illustrated in *The Studio*, November 1893, p. 57.

execution, he apparently insists upon the dotted ornament being worked out by means of single dots instead of dotted gouges, for we cannot think that such an accomplished workman as Mr Maullen or his experienced employer, Mr Zaehnsdorf, would have chosen single dots as preferable to dotted gouges for working out these designs, but for positive instructions to do so. The work is more expensive but less perfect'. Probably here, with the use of the single dot tool. which is such anathema to the reviewer, we may sense the first stirrings of a movement which was eventually to lead away from the formal stylized designs of the past to the greater freedom of design of modern bindings. Without seeing the particular volumes, there is perhaps more than a suspicion that this report is biassed against the non-trade binders and designers.

Bindings for Lady Dilke

The South Kensington Museum Library, which later became the National Art Library, or Victoria and Albert Museum Library, has been mentioned as the source of the pattern for the art-workmen's competition. Its large collection of bookbindings contains several examples of Zaehnsdorf work, and includes three examples from the library of Lady Dilke.

Lady Dilke is perhaps not now so well remembered as her second husband, Sir Charles Wentworth Dilke, Bart.* She was a historian of French art and the author of several treatises, and some volumes of short stories. She directed that on her death (which took place on 24 October 1904) her valuable jewels and collection of art books, Aldines and Elzevirs should pass to the Victoria and Albert Museum. Two of her Zaehnsdorf bindings, now in the Library of the Museum, are decorated with a pattern of stamps of the cypher 'EFSD' (Emilia Francis Strong Dilke)† which, according to a pencilled note in one of the volumes, had been designed by Lady Dilke.

---

* Both Sir Charles, and Lady Dilke are the subject of memoirs in *Dictionary of National Biography*.
† The memoir on Lady Dilke explains that her second Christian name was Francis, given after her godfather.

Binding, 1895, for Lady Dilke, of
Figure del Vecchio, Nuovo, Testamento (160 × 110mm)
(Courtesy Board of Trustees, Victoria & Albert Museum)

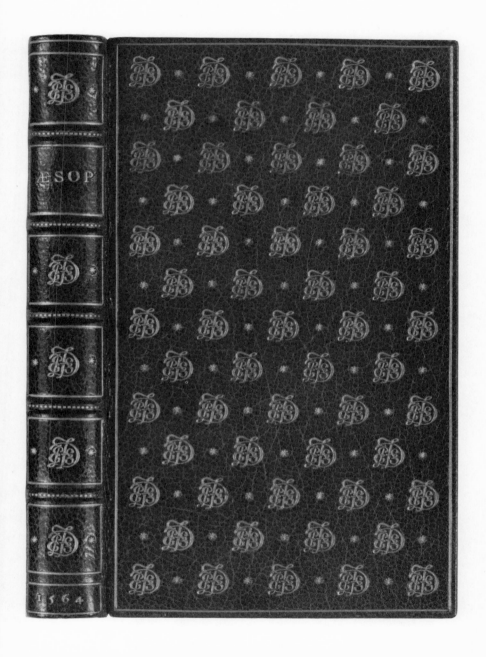

Binding for Lady Dilke, of *Aesopi Phrygia Alioren Fabula* (125 × 77mm)
(Courtesy Board of Trustees, Victoria & Albert Museum)

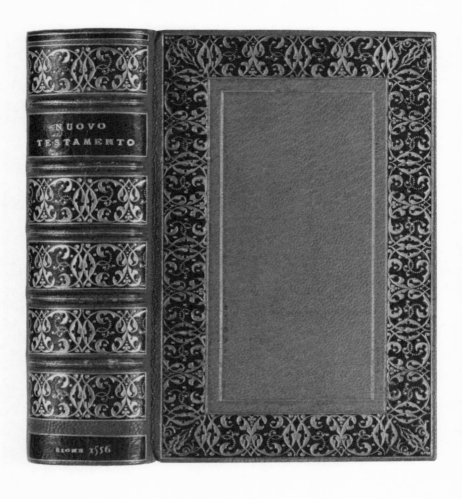

Binding for Lady Dilke, of *Il Nuovo ed Eterno Testamento* (120 × 85mm)
(Courtesy Board of Trustees, Victoria & Albert Museum)

One of these bindings, in red morocco, is stamped on the front turn-in 'BOUND BY ZAEHNSDORF 1895', and is on *Figure del Vecchio, Nuovo Testamento*, printed at Lyons in 1554 and 1559 respectively [press-mark RC.C.11]. The other binding decorated with this stamp is on *Aesopi Phrygis Alioren Fabula*, Lyons 1564 [press-mark 88.D.39] and is in brown morocco, again signed by Zaehnsdorf on the front turn-in, but without any date. This second binding has the note that the stamp was designed by Lady Dilke. The third example of a Zaehnsdorf binding from the library of Lady Dilke and now in the Victoria and Albert Museum is on a New Testament, *Il Nuovo Ed Eterno Testamento*, printed at Lyons in 1556 [press-mark RC.D.21]. This is in citron coloured morocco with a broad inlay of black morocco round the sides and in panels of the back, upon which an effective scheme of gold-tooled ornament is worked, the edges are gilt in the rough, and the binding is enclosed in a morocco covered drop case. It is signed by means of an inked stamp, and in addition it carries the Zaehnsdorf medallic mark on the inside rear board. This mark is a small oval tool apparently used, along with other similar stamps, as a quality mark on the superior bindings produced by the firm. It represents the medieval apprentice seated at the sewing frame and is taken from the wood engraving of a binder's shop by Jost Amman, which Zaehnsdorf's used in their advertising and on their stationery and was also used by J. W. Zaehnsdorf and Ernest Zaehnsdorf as the basis of their bookplates, which are discussed in Appendix D. The following illustration reproduces three of these tools still in the possession of the company but now somewhat rather worn by frequent use; also shown are three name pallets as used to sign bindings.

ZÆHNSDORF LTD.   BOUND BY ZAEHNSDORF, LONDON

BOUND BY ZAEHNSDORF, LONDON

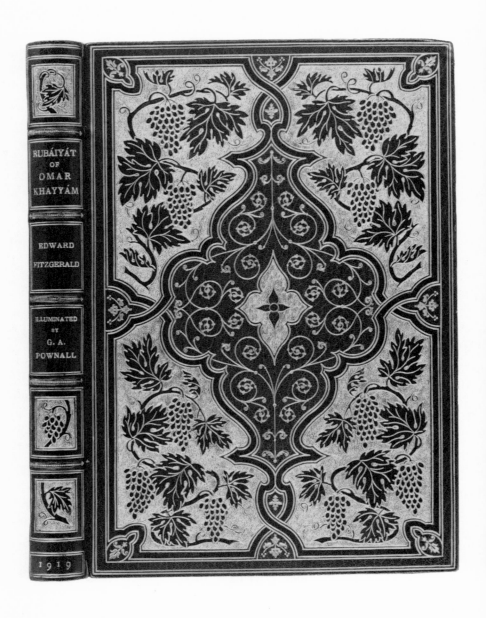

Binding, 1920, of *Omar Khayyam* (293 × 205mm)
(Courtesy Board of Trustees, Victoria & Albert Museum)

A Binding of 1920

Another binding in the Victoria and Albert Museum Library, not having any connection with Lady Dilke, emanates from the period following the First World War, since it was bound in 1920. This binding points back to the earlier binding of *Sakoontala*, in both the subject matter of the book and the style of binding, although now considerably less lavish. This is a binding of a manuscript of *Omar Khayyam*, which was written and illuminated in 1919 by Gilbert A. Pownall [press-mark KRP.A.35]. The binding is signed and dated, and is of blue morocco with an oriental style design of arabesques and bunches of grapes and vine leaves inlaid in coloured leathers and gilt. The doublures are of watered silk. This volume was given to the V & A in 1951 by Miss Kate Burney, who sent a letter to Zaehnsdorfs which she had received from Arthur Wheen, Keeper of the Library, in which he described it as 'a welcome addition to the Library'.

Testimonial Volumes

A source of work for the firm, in the last decades of the previous century and the early years of the present one, was the production of addresses and testimonial volumes for presentation to public figures to mark some special event or anniversary, and various specimen leaves for collecting signatures and typical addresses are preserved in the records. Among the more interesting items of Zaehnsdorf work of this type are testimonials for Cardinal Manning, the address presented to Queen Victoria by the Actors and Managers of Great Britain in 1887, the address to the King on his Coronation in 1902, and the address to Sir Henry Irving on his knighthood.

For Manning's elevation to the dignity of a Cardinal in 1875, no less than three separate volumes were produced, of varying degrees of elaboration in their binding. For the finest two of these records still exist, showing the cost of materials, workmen's time and profit margins. The largest of these volumes measured 38 × 28 inches (96 × 71 cm), it was described as a 'Blank Book to paste Testimonials in, for Cardinal Manning. Red Morocco Inlaid, Gilt Edges, 50 Leaves'. It has not proved possible to trace this book, so its magnificence may only be guessed at from the expenditure of time and materials — finishing 14 days and 400 gold leaves used! The detailed costs (copied from a Zaehnsdorf ledger) and totalling £30, for this job were:

1875	£	s	d
100 Sheets Paper	2	5	0
50 do Plate paper		15	0
Pasting together 100 Sheets			
Pressing Paper			
Guarding & getting up for sewing	2	14	0
Sewing		2	6
forwarding, 3 days		18	0
End papers		2	6
Millboards		7	6
Gilting Edges		10	0
3 Skins Morocco 13/6	2	2	0
Headbanding		2	0
Covering & joints		15	0
Inlaying and Morocco		7	6
finishing 14 days	7	0	0
400 Gold	1	0	0
Sundries		7	6
Addending [sic] 4 times at the Cardinal	1	10	0
2 Men at Work at his house 3 days	1	16	0
	£22	14	6
Profitt [sic]	7	5	6
	£30	0	0

The second volume, also in red morocco, with the arms of the Cardinal inlaid, and silver bosses at the corners of each cover, and measuring 12¼ × 9½ inches (310 × 240 mm),

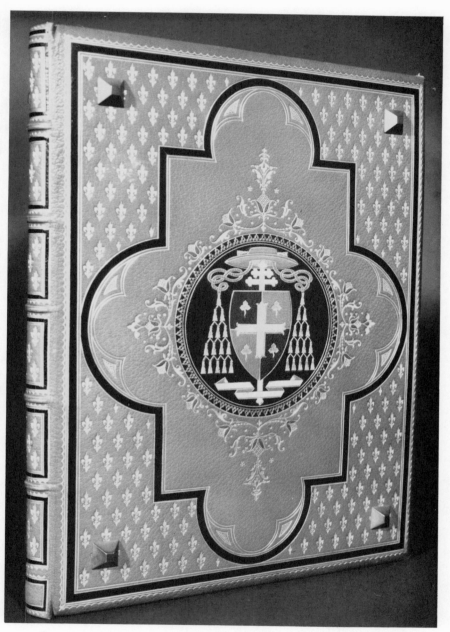

Testimonial Volume, 1875, for Cardinal Manning (310 × 240mm)
(Courtesy His Eminence Cardinal Hume)

contains the signatures of the clergy, secular and regular, of the Diocese of Westminster. The binding has been maintained in good condition by its box, which is fitted with a strut to support the box at an angle to display the volume, and it is now with the archives at Archbishop's House Westminster. The costs for this binding, totalling £13.15s. (£13.75), which is obviously less sumptuous than the one mentioned previously, are given in the Zaehnsdorf ledger as:

1875	Red Morocco		

Testimonial for Cardinal Manning
4to Size, Illuminated on Vellum single leaves.
8 Silver Bosses and Case.

Squaring & getting up		1	6
Sewing & headbanding		1	0
Millboards		1	6
forwarding		4	6
Gilting Edges		2	6
Interleaving Paper		1	0
Morocco		8	6
Covering & Joints		5	6
finishing 70 hours	3	10	0
Morocco for Inlaying		5	0
Silk for Ends		8	6
Lehrich for fitting Silk		4	0
Sundries		2	6
8 Silver Bosses	2	10	0
Case, Silk Lined		15	0
	9	1	0
Profit for Work & Addending [sic] to several Gentl.	4	14	0
	£15	15	0

The third volume contains the signatures of the laity, and measures 13 × 9¾ inches (330 × 250 mm), and it, too, is at Archbishop's House. It is a simpler binding than the previous one, and not having a protective case is not nearly so well preserved. The comparison of the condition of these two volumes provides a graphic example of the value of cases for conservation and justification for the 15s. (75p) spent on the case. This binding, like the previous one, is signed by Zaehnsdorf, but no mention of it is to be found in the firm's records.

Another address to Cardinal Manning, which Zaehnsdorf carried out, in 1890, was for the twenty-fifth anniversary of his Episcopal consecration and was from the Jewish Community. The execution of this address probably depended more on the skill of the cabinet maker, rather than that of the bookbinder. It was an address and frame enclosed in an ebony case with folding doors and its dimensions are given as, over seven feet (2.1 m) in height and about four feet (1.2 m) in breadth. In spite of its size it has not proved possible to locate this artefact, and the information about it is from a special edition of *The Jewish Chronicle*, dated 31 October 1890, which includes a description, by the Honorary Secretary, Mr Isidore Spielman, of the Testimonial Committee:

The Address, which has been most carefully executed by Mr Zaehnsdorf, bears at the foot, the Signatures of the leading men of the Jewish Community in this Country, who have been associated in Communal work with Cardinal Manning.

The vellum is surrounded by a framework of pale brown Russia Leather, upon which is a handsome border in the Rococo style, relieved at various sections by inlaid leather-work of brighter hues. Around the bevel of this framework has been impressed in gold . . . texts in Hebrew and English . . .

At the four corners are the Arms of the Cardinal, and David's Shield.

The Address and Frame are enclosed in an Ebony Case with folding doors, the panels of which are lined with red leather richly embossed in gold, with the cardinal's hat and the double triangle. In the centre of one panel, the Arms of His Eminence have been richly inlaid in leathers of various colours, and David's Shield on the other. These panels are surrounded by a decorated border of palm branches, artistically executed in gold.

The doors of this massive Ebony Case are carved with the Cardinal's monogram and the date of presentation.

The whole is surmounted with the Arms of His Eminence, carved in solid ebony, . . .

Some idea of the magnitude of this work may be gathered from its size; viz. 7 feet high, by 4 feet wide.

F

Ebony Cabinet enclosing address, 1890, for Cardinal Manning

The good taste, workmanship and artistic effect, reflect high credit upon Mr. Zaehnsdorf of Cambridge Circus, Shaftesbury Avenue, in whose care the order for this unique address was placed.

In spite of the comment that this production relied more on the cabinet maker than the bookbinder, it is clear from the above description that the bookbinders' skills were used extensively: for the vellum of the address itself and the pale brown Russia leather framework, for the inlaid leather of various colours, for the texts impressed in gold, and the decorated border.

The Jubilee Address to Queen Victoria from the Actors and Managers of the United Kingdom on the attainment of the fiftieth year of her reign in 1887, must have been an important commission, in view of the historic occasion and the sumptuousness of the volume. In addition to the illuminated address there were nearly two hundred sheets of vellum each decorated with a water colour framing design and containing the signatures of every actor in the land. The binding was in red morocco, tooled with a design of scrolls, and according to the Jubilee Celebration number of *The Graphic*, of 28 June 1887, 'it has been declared by many experts to be one of the finest specimens of the beautiful art of bookbinding seen in recent years.'

Zaehnsdorfs were responsible for producing similar but less lavish volumes: for Sir Henry Irving in 1895 when he received his knighthood, the first actor ever to be so honoured; and in 1901 the Address to the Throne to be presented by the Actors and Managers to King Edward VII on his coronation, in 1902.

Loyal Rulers and Leaders of the East

Publishing was an occasional activity of Zaehnsdorfs, and over the years they published a few volumes of specialised interest. The volume of Miss Prideaux's reprinted articles on bookbinding, published by Zaehnsdorf in 1903, has already been mentioned; other volumes did not have the same relevance to their main activity. In 1897 they published the

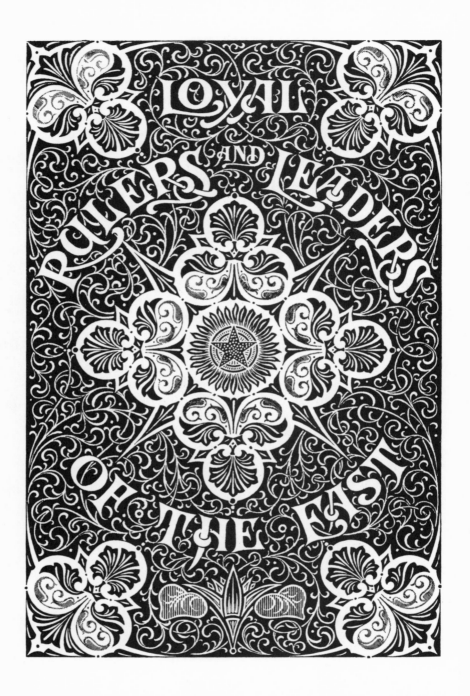

Block for cover of *Loyal Rulers and Leaders of the East* (204 × 139mm)

List of Members of the Royal Yacht Squadron and their Yachts from its Foundation in 1815 to 1897, compiled by Montague Guest, Librarian of the Royal Yacht Squadron. This was bound in white buckram with the emblem of the Royal Yacht Squadron in gold on the front cover. A later edition, covering the years 1898–1931, compiled by Sir John C. E. Shelley-Rolls, Bart, was published in 1932. A more ostentatious production was *Loyal Rulers and Leaders of the East*, published in 1922, and edited by the Earl of Carnwath, assisted by a Supervisory Committee of which R. H. Shaw, a director of Zaehnsdorf, was Chairman. The introduction to the volume was by Field Marshal Earl Haig. The intention of this work was to place on permanent record the service to the Empire, in the provision of men, materials, and money, rendered through the Great War by the ruling princes and other potentates and leaders in the East. It was issued in two bindings, one of blue cloth and a superior binding in leather. The design of this latter binding was discussed in some detail by Thomas Harrison in a lecture on 'Book Designing' given to the Printing, Bookbinding and Kindred Trades Overseer's Association which was reported in *The British and Colonial Printer and Stationer* of 3 May 1923.

Referring to the design, Harrison said that in order to befit the subject matter of the book the design was to be a Western tribute to the beauty and glory of Eastern decorative art. He approached his task by studying many books containing examples of Eastern art, and for a considerable time looking at nothing else, so that he became steeped in the subject. It was a problem to provide lettering with the necessary Eastern atmosphere by adapting Western letters. This was overcome by introducing letters with a semi-gothic treatment in order to give the required balance and a rich decorative effect. This binding was mentioned by Ernest Zaehnsdorf in his lecture to the Stationers' Company when he described it as a unique example of modern blocked work, of great interest to the bookbinding craftsman, and illustrating the combination of high technical ideals with commercial requirements. The block for the cover of *Loyal Rulers and Leaders of the East* is still retained by the company.

Queen Mary's Dolls' House

The binding of small books appears to have had an especial fascination for Ernest Zaehnsdorf. He usually mentioned this topic in his lectures, and he referred to miniature bindings in both his Stationers' Company lecture and in his broadcast talk. In a letter published in *The Daily Mail* on 18 February 1922, he stated that the smallest book which he had ever bound was in morocco, tooled in gold, weighed 26½ grains (1.7g), and measured 45/64 × 25/64 in. (18 × 10 mm). He also referred to the binding of volumes for Queen Mary's Dolls' House, which he said did not represent an effort to produce 'the smallest book', but were to the scale of 1/12, resulting in books which were about one inch tall.

In view of this interest in small bindings, the opportunity to bind some of the volumes for the Library of Queen Mary's Dolls' House would be a welcome challenge for Ernest Zaehnsdorf. The concept of this dolls' house arose in 1920 with a suggestion that a present should be made to H. M. Queen Mary of as complete a model of a twentieth-century residence as could be contrived, with everything being to a scale of one-twelfth. The library contained some two hundred books written in their authors' own hands, in addition there were about seventy miscellaneous, reference, and printed books. The binding of these books was the work of several firms, all of whom gave their services, including, Birdsall & Son, Robert Riviere & Son, Sangorski and Sutcliffe, and Zaehnsdorf Limited. One of the bindings by Zaehnsdorf was a *Bradshaw's Railway Guide*, specially printed to one-twelfth scale, that is, 1⁷⁄₁₆ × 1³⁄₁₆ in. (36 × 30 mm). This book, together with the miniature laying press and plough used for the forwarding of the volumes, was exhibited at Ernest Zaehnsdorf's Stationers' Hall Lecture. Another of these bindings, by the company, was on Michael Sadleir's *A Picture of Morvane* (which is the original draft of the opening chapter of his novel *Desolate Splendour*). This is illustrated by E. V. Lucas in his, *The Book of the Queen's Dolls' House Library* (1924). The names of the Zaehnsdorf binders responsible for these bindings were given as W. Bowyer, G. Molyneaux and G. Page.

Bindings of the 1920s and 1930s

A binding dated 1920 on a manuscript of *Omar Khayyam* has been described, and it followed the tradition of Zaehnsdorf bindings of the past. Only limited evidence is available to indicate the styles of bookbinding which the company produced under Ernest Zaehnsdorf. At the exhibition, which accompanied his first public lecture, were two bindings which were described as picture work. One was a binding on the poems of Thomas Hardy, on which a portrait of the author was reproduced in leather. The other was a binding of *Alice in Wonderland*, showing the Mad Hatter after a drawing by Tenniel.

During the early 1930s book covers were being produced whose designs attempted to be symbolic of the contents, and also, in some instances, to express something of the owner's personality. This was a definite departure from the more usual type of binding which generally had little, if any, relation to the subject matter of the book. *The British and Colonial Printer and Stationer* for 22 December 1932 carried a short article on 'Symbolism in Bookbinding Design — Striking a Modern Note'. After a brief discussion of the requirements for a binding to reflect the personality of the person for whom it is being bound, a recent binding by Messrs Zaehnsdorf Limited was illustrated and described. It was stated that the company had had recently produced several bindings along these lines, and the binding selected was of a Library Catalogue for an American sportsman, and reference was made to the delicately varied colours of the levant morocco leather used. The photograph showed a highly pictorial binding of a landscape panel with trees, three human figures, a horse, two hounds, antique pistol, hockey stick, and tennis racquet. Certainly a bold attempt to shake off the shackles of the past.

Some six months later, the same trade periodical, in its issue of 6 July 1933, reviewed the Exhibition of British Industrial Art being held at Dorland House, Lower Regent Street, London, with the encouragement of the Board of Trade. Whilst in general the reviewer found no great originality in the designs of the fine bindings, he did single out Zaehnsdorfs for 'some interesting essays in modernity', and referred to their binding of *Pablo Picasso* as 'an attempt to give a rendering of the artist's style in a pattern of morocco leather inlays.'

Four weeks later, on 3 August 1933, *The British and Colonial Printer and Stationer*, returned to 'Symbolism in Bookbinding', referring specifically to the work of Mr R. P. Sleeman, who, after obtaining experience in colour poster work in the North of England, had joined Messrs Zaehnsdorf during 1932 to assist them with designing colour composition for bookbindings. A statement from Mr Sleeman of his views on these designs was quoted, where in conclusion he gave the aim as being the production of 'an harmonised construction in which covers, end-papers and book are a real co-ordinated unit, and never a haphazard collection.' Whilst this statement of aim would be accepted by today's designers of contemporary bindings, it is doubtful if the two examples of his symbolic style of binding — a *Gulliver's Travels*, and a menu book, would be so acceptable. However, the pictorial designs of a figure of Gulliver, and a glass of wine and a lobster, both inlaid in appropriately coloured leather, again show a determination to give a 'modern' treatment to bookbinding.

5

Conservation and Restoration

No discussion of the activities of Zaehnsdorfs would be complete without mention of their work in the field of conservation and restoration of books and documents. They were preeminent in this area from the early days of the firm and cuttings preserved in their records relating to paper cleaning, book worm and similar topics show evidence of this interest. There are also samples of paper before and after cleaning, showing a remarkable improvement in appearance and no deleterious effects after the lapse of a century. Unfortunately no details of the methods adopted are present. J. W. Zaehnsdorf's membership of the Society of Arts Committee on Leather for bookbinding at the beginning of this century, and the employment by the company of a staff research chemist in the early 1930s, show a continuing interest and growing involvement with the increasing scientific understanding of the processes concerned with deterioration and conservation.

A number of important public authorities, institutions and private individuals entrusted Zaehnsdorfs with the repair of valuable books and documents in their possession. Thomas J. Wise, in his correspondence with John Henry Wrenn,* makes several references to specially fitted cases by Zaehnsdorf, as a means of protecting original boards and paper covers. An undated newspaper cutting in the files refers to an exhibition at the York Street premises (i.e. between 1873 and 1890) of many ancient records of the Corporation of Winchester, some dating back to 1349. It describes the skilful way in which repairs have been made to damaged parchments, and the manner in which the crumbled fragments of many of the

* *Letters of Thomas J. Wise to John Henry Wrenn,* Edited by Fannie E. Ratchford. New York (1944).

records have been carefully and securely interleaved in substantially bound folio volumes which permit easy reference.

A letter dated 7 March 1877 from Government House, Bermuda, thanks Joseph Zaehnsdorf for binding the records of the Colony of Bermuda. Accounts exist for the expenditure of time and materials on this work and two subsequent commissions which, during a period of somewhat over a year, occupied a substantial proportion of the time of some of Zaehnsdorf's workmen, especially one named Chandler. The undated entry for this work is:

Sir J. H. Lefroy.

Colonial Record of Bermuda
3 Vols, Mended, Sized & Mended
Marocco [sic] plain lettd interleaved.

Chandler 280 hours mending			
& sizing	14	10	0
Tissue paper for mending		3	9
Best Whatman Bank Note			
Paper for strengthening		7	6
do Strong Paper for			
Interleaving		15	6
do Imperial		12	6
3 Reams Blotting Paper	2	9	6
2 Reams Cartridge	1	8	0
Index Paper ruled		4	0
Sundries		7	6
Binding in Marocco			
3 Vols @ 32/6 & 35/–	5	0	0
	£25	18	3
	£30	0	0

Work on a further four volumes of these records was costed on 15 December 1877, and showed Chandler being occupied for five weeks at a cost of £13. 5. 0 (£13.25), and requiring 7lb of glue (3.2 kg) at 5/– (25p), writing a contents list was charged at £4, and binding the four volumes was £7. The total cost for time and materials was £31. 9. 6 (£31. 47½), which with sundries and profit at £6. 10. 6 (£6. 52½) gave a total of £38.

This work must have proved satisfactory, since another seven volumes followed. Again the records are interesting as showing the time and materials required for such a commission. Chandler was heavily involved, his time being 13 weeks. There was a large usage of glue [for sizing], and blotting paper [for drying the records after washing]. The complete account is:

Sir J. H. Lefroy
27/4/78 Colonial Record of Bermuda
            7 Vols. Mended, Sized & Mended
        Marrocco [*sic*] plain lettd & interleaved
Time

Chandler	13 weeks	2.12.6	34. 2.6
James	2 Days 1 hour		10.6
Ben	6 Days 7 hours		1.13.6
William	Sizing 7 Days		1.15.0
Rothe	pasting 3 Days		18.0

Materials

4 Reams Blotting paper 11/6	2. 2.0
16 Quires Common D. Cartridge	10.6
16 Quires Tissue paper	15.0
10½ Quire Whatmans Wire	1.10.0
10½ Quire Bank Paper	1. 5.0
12½ Quire Tone Paper⎤ Inter	
15½ Quire Tone Paper⎦ leaving	1. 1.0
25 Quire Bank Paper	3. 0.0
21 Sheets Ruled Paper for Index	1.8
14 lb of Glue	10.0
Starch and Sundries	15.4
4 Vols 20⅛ × 14½ @44/–	8.16.0
3 Vols 17½ × 11 @35/–	5. 5.0
Profit	11.18.0

[The book-keeper had trouble in totalling this entry and after several alterations an incorrect final figure of £78.13.0 (£78.65) was obtained. It should have been £76.9.0 (£76.45).]

One of the foremost collectors of manuscripts relating to Yorkshire was Richard Frank of Campsall, who died in 1769. In 1875 Zaehnsdorf undertook a small commission for his descendant Bacon Frank, who wrote from Campsall Hall, Doncaster, on 8 December 1875, saying that he was much pleased with the way in which the binding of his MSS. had been done. On 6 December 1881, the Reform Club were

quoted prices for repairing books ranging from 3/– (15p) for
demy 8vo to 8/6 (42½p) if lettered, and if gilt, from 3/6 (17½p)
to 10/6 (52½p), for the same sizes.

Such work continued to form an important part of the firm's
activities; on 13 October 1933 the Comptroller of the Corporation of London wrote saying that the restoration of the Bridge
House Records had been carried out in a very satisfactory
manner. During the intervening period Zaehnsdorfs had
undertaken, free of charge, using skins supplied by E. & J.
Richardson of Newcastle-on-Tyne, the repair of the flood
damaged records of the parish of St Clement's with St
Edmund's, in Norwich. Why this particular disaster should
have resulted in a donation of skill and time from Zaehnsdorf
and leather from Richardson is not now known. The circumstances are that during the last week of August 1912, heavy
rainfall over England and Wales resulted in extensive flood-
ing in many places. On 26 August a 'cloudburst' at Norwich
resulted in 6 inches (15 cm) of rain from 4 am to 3.15 pm. *The
Times* of 2 September 1912 carried a brief report of the flood
damage in Norfolk, together with an appeal from the Lord
Mayor of Norwich for assistance for the relief of the victims.
Perhaps, to suggest a base motive, Zaehnsdorf may have
sensed the opportunity of bringing his services to the notice of
the church authorities, who might then subsequently turn to
him for restoration work on their many records. Perhaps, too,
the chance to work on flood-damaged records, and the consequent opportunity of increasing his store of knowledge and
practical experience, appealed to his enquiring mind.

Some speedy remedial action was obviously undertaken on
the then current registers, since the Rector wrote to Zaehnsdorf on 18 September 1912, thanking him for the two registers
which had been returned and commenting that the work had
been carried out beautifully, such that they seemed better
than before the flood, and wondering how they would manage
with the really bad ones. Amongst some general information
about the effects of the floods, he passes on the thanks of his
wife to Zaehnsdorf for recommending formaldehyde solution
for deodorizing. The Parish Magazine, *Fellowship*, for October 1912, gave an account of the flood and its aftermath,

during the course of which it referred to, 'two names to which it is only just that acknowledgement should be made. Mr Joseph Zaehnsdorf, of Shaftesbury Avenue, London, the King's bookbinder, most generously offered free of charge to repair, so far as possible, the damage done to the valuable registers of the two churches. The registers date back to 1538, and the iron safe in which they were kept was under water for about a day and a half. The water got in through the keyhole, and the books and documents when got out were little better, for the most part, than a mass of pulp. Then Messrs E. & J. Richardson, Elswick Leather Works, Newcastle-on-Tyne, very kindly contributed a number of skins for the purpose of rebinding the registers when they shall have been repaired. To both these firms our most grateful thanks are due. Two of the registers have already come back and present splendid examples of the bookbinder's art.' All the volumes repaired had a label inserted in them referring to the generosity of the

St. CLEMENT with St. EDMUND
—————— NORWICH ——————

THIS REGISTER WAS INJURED IN THE EAST ANGLIAN FLOOD OF 1912 AND WAS REPAIRED BY J. ZAEHNSDORF OF LONDON AS A HELP OFFERING
℃ THE LEATHER FOR THE BINDING OF THIS BOOK WAS PRESENTED BY E. & J. RICHARDSON OF NEWCASTLE-ON-TYNE

Label inserted in books repaired after the 1912 flood

two firms. On 15 April 1913, the Bishop of Norwich wrote to the Rector, thanking him for information about the adventures of the church books during the floods, and of the great kindness of Messrs Zaehnsdorf and Messrs Richardson and asking that they be informed how all appreciated their sympathy and friendliness and generosity.

91

A further aid to those responsible for the care of fine bindings was the book leather preservative which the company supplied for many years, under the name of Hutchins 'Curator'. The publicity brochure for this product stated that it was 'the result of forty years unceasing research work by Mr Hutchins, late Keeper of the Gennadius Collection'. His joint paper with Ernest Zaehnsdorf on 'The Preservation of Leather Bindings' in the *American Book Collector* of January 1932, has already been mentioned, with its reference to the availability of a composition whose preparation was too difficult for the amateur. J. W. Zaehnsdorf had served on the Society of Arts Committee on Leather for Bookbinding, at the beginning of the century, and his son served on the later Bookbinding Leather Committee of the British Leather Manufacturers' Association; so the principals of the company kept in touch with, and helped to direct, developments in this important field. Statements made in support of the Hutchins 'Curator' leather preservative, warning against beeswax and advocating the use of animal fats followed by a thin elastic veneer varnish, are not at variance with the results of present-day research into the prevention of deterioration of leather bindings.

Further evidence of the company's thinking in the scientific aspects of restoration is given by a brochure dated 1932, *A New Outlook on the Cleaning and Restoration of Books, Colour Prints and Drawings: the results of a scientific investigation.* After referring to the methods for cleaning paper of the previous fifty years — permanganate, sulphurous acid, chloride of lime and hydrogen peroxide, and all noted for the difficulty of their complete removal, even after prolonged washing — a new technique is suggested. This is the use of a completely volatile agent, stated to be capable of removing all stains without damage and making it possible in many cases to treat a book without unbinding. Although a really effective and reliable volatile treatment is still not available today, the efforts of more than half-a-century ago merit the claim 'we feel a certain pride that the House of Zaehnsdorf once more leads the way'.

APPENDIX A

Dispute
of September 1872

The following list is of the nineteen workmen who left the employ of Joseph Zaehnsdorf on 28 September 1872, over his employment of non-Society men and foreigners; it was prepared from information given in his private notebook on employees. Also shown is the nature of their employment and length of service with Zaehnsdorf, and weekly wages.

Aggersbury	forwarder	–	33/–*
Barrington	extra finisher	15 years	48/–
Burton	extra finisher	5 years	42/–
Collins	forwarder	10 years	32/–
Crockett Senr	forwarder	several years	32/–
Crump	–	3 months	32/–
Francis	extra finisher	3 months	40/–
Genth	extra finisher	13 years	48/–
Greenfield	–	18–20 months	33/–
Jackson	finisher	2 months	40/–
Langford	forwarder	some time	32/–
Locker	assistant finisher	7 years	30/–
Mills	collater	20 years	32/–
Mundy	forwarder	–	32/–
Munkow	assistant forwarder	–	24/–
Rowlinson	forwarder	–	33/–
Sanderson	extra forwarder	–	36/–
Simpson	foreman	16 years	40/–
Shepherd	forwarder	–	20/–

('old man helped at anything')

*Amounts quoted in shillings, or one-twentieth of a pound sterling.

APPENDIX B

The Binding of a Book

In July 1890 Zaehnsdorfs issued a small brochure to coincide with their move to Shaftesbury Avenue, entitled, *The Binding of a Book*. In addition to a short introduction mentioning the new premises and several pages of advertising matter, there was a description of the various processes involved in binding a book, eleven rules for prolonging the life of a book and its binding, and six wood-engraved illustrations of binding operatives and a short definition of their work.

An extended version of this brochure, printed at the Chiswick Press, was issued in 1895 under the title, *A Short History of Bookbinding*. This had a coloured frontispiece of a Zaehnsdorf binding and contained a short history of bookbinding, a glossary of styles and terms including nine illustrations of binding operations (six being from, or based on those of the first version, but slightly enlarged). A brief mention of the premises and services offered was followed by five photographs of the Cambridge Works at Shaftesbury Avenue, each on a page of advertising. A reprint was issued in 1913, following the registration of the company, but the title page still carried the original date of 1895. The design of the cover had been modified and the illustration used on it was the composite of the Jost Amman cuts of the binderies as used for the Zaehnsdorf book plate, the two previous brochures having used the single figure seated at the sewing frame. The date given on the cover was 1913, and it carried the new style of the company, Zaehnsdorf Ltd. This reprint had no frontispiece, otherwise its contents were identical with the first issue.

The wood-engraved illustrations used in these brochures were typical of their period and were ideal for their purpose, of explaining the binding of a book to potential customers. The illustrations from the first brochure, are shown opposite.

Collator and Sewer

Forwarder and Headbander

Coverer and Finisher

Illustrations from *The Binding of a Book*

In 1907, *The Art Journal* carried an article (pp. 137–147) by R. E. D. Sketchley on 'Book-Bindings'. This surveyed and illustrated the work of many binders, including Zaehnsdorf, Riviere, Leighton, Sangorski and Sutcliffe, the Oxford University Press, Ramage, W. H. Smith, and also Alice Pattinson, Mary E. Robinson, and Jessie King. Zaehnsdorfs had part of this article reprinted, as a pamphlet in an edition of 600 copies. This contained the opening paragraphs, which briefly outlined the development of bookbinding in England and extolled the work of the firm. The eight photographs of bindings attributed to J. W. Zaehnsdorf, from the original article, were also reprinted, and accompanied by an additional photograph of a Zaehnsdorf binding.

By Special Appointment to
H.R.H. the Prince of Wales.

Highest Awards,
London, Paris, Chicago, &c.

ZAEHNSDORF,

CAMBRIDGE WORKS,

144–146 SHAFTESBURY AVENUE, W.C.

ARTISTIC BOOKBINDING.

Post Free, "SHORT HISTORY OF BOOKBINDING."

A Zaehnsdorf Advertisement, in *The Portfolio, c.* 1897

APPENDIX C

'The Romance of Bookbinding'

The following is the text of a broadcast talk delivered on Saturday 12 May 1923, by Mr E. J. W. Zaehnsdorf, from the London Broadcasting Station of the British Broadcasting Company. It was printed in The British and Colonial Printer and Stationer, *of 17 May 1923.*

To the bookbinder credit must be given to a very large degree for the preservation of our national records, whether printed or written. Mankind has always endeavoured to pass to posterity accounts of his daily life, his discoveries and his beliefs. In France and Spain there are some caves which have drawings on the walls, drawn in the Stone Age, depicting hunting scenes and other daily occupations, which give us a clear idea of exactly how the hunt was conducted, the number of animals chased, and the resulting 'bag'.

For written accounts we must turn to the East. In Babylon some 3,000 to 4,000 years ago men recorded their affairs on clay, which was afterwards baked, and, to preserve the record, it was sometimes enclosed in an outer envelope of baked clay, which was also inscribed, so that, should the envelope be broken, the contents still stood a chance of passing on the valued information. Such tablets may be seen in the British Museum and afford the earliest instance of the duty of a bookbinder.

The Romans used wooden tablets about ¼ inch thick, in the centre of which hot wax was poured and allowed to harden. The wax was scratched with a pointed iron stylus (the forerunner of our modern stylographic pen); the other end was flattened, so that it might be used to erase errors, or perhaps to remove the whole of the writing. Two or more such tablets were sometimes strung together with brass wire rings, just like some of our modern loose-leaf pocket books, and in this way we have a very early form of our modern book.

Herodotus, the historian (b. 484 B.C.), mentions that some of his writing was on the skins of animals. This fairly gives a date to the introduction of vellum — a material that has been in use ever since, and even today vellum is used for documents and deeds and special forms of address. In Roman times books written on vellum were rolled up for storing in the library, which must have presented a very different appearance from the modern public library.

The Ancient Egyptians made use of the split stalk of the papyrus, a reed which grows on the banks of the Nile. Three layers of the split stalk were mounted together until a length of some 15 or 20 feet was reached. On this they wrote their hieroglyphics, and specimens may be seen in the British Museum.

Paper was first made by the Chinese thousands of years ago. The date of its introduction into England is a matter of speculation; but it was used extensively in Mediæval times, and assumed great importance on the introduction of printing in the 15th century.

The binding of Church missals and books of devotion was a special feature of monastic life, and considerable craft skill was displayed by the monks in binding their books. Their knowledge of the requirements of a bound book was of the highest, and they solved the problem so well that even today we practically copy the methods as practised in the eighth and ninth centuries.

The principles of the binding of a modern novel, though done by machinery, are based on the old monkish ideals.

The reason why we bind a book is to preserve it and afford protection. A printed bundle of sheets of paper would quickly come to grief, some would be lost, dust and dirt would ruin the leaves, and general confusion would prevail. So the bookbinder comes to the rescue, and suitably binds the leaves together, and thus ensures the preservation demanded.

In ancient times vellum was frequently used for the cover, but morocco (goat skin) was a great favourite; sometimes asses' skin was employed, and during the 16th and 17th centuries binders covered the volumes in calf skin. Today, for the best work, we use carefully selected morocco.

Books have many enemies such as fire and water: Louvain is an instance which immediately comes to mind, but every year the fire demon takes his toll from private homes and many beautifully bound books are destroyed.

Religion has in the past persecuted books, and public bonfires, supervised by the public hangman, have been made by religious opponents. The Mahomedans, for instance, held that if a book agreed with the Koran, it was superfluous, and if it disagreed, it was heretical and should be destroyed.

Another enemy is spring cleaning. In the annual spring clean many valuable books have been exchanged as waste paper for a fern or an aspidistra. I have heard even of an instance where the poor books had their covers ruthlessly washed with soap and water. Children are innocent enemies of books, and with paintbox or crayon, or perhaps scissors and scrapbook, have done incalculable damage. A typical instance is the first edition of *Alice in Wonderland*. This book is always soiled and the picture of the Mad Hatter's Tea Party is a favourite picture for children to love in an embarrassing manner in a book worth about £50.

Bookworms do great damage to books, and you may remember Professor Lefroy's lecture to you on the damage to the roof of Westminster Hall by the grub of the Death Watch. The Death Watch will attack books, but the little fellow that especially marks books for his feast is somewhat similar in appearance and rejoices in the Latin name of *Anobium Striatium*. The repair of worm eaten books by a bookbinder is a difficult task, but frequently undertaken and the damage repaired in an invisible manner comparable with the feat of repairing the roof of Westminster Hall.

Books have been bound in curious materials such as a portion of an elephant's ear, or the skin of an animal, lion or tiger, shot on a hunting expedition.

During the War the British prisoners at Ruhleben caught rats and used the skins to bind books, and, though not professional bookbinders, did the work most creditably and proved the triumph of British resource over depressing difficulties.

The most uncanny book I have ever handled was covered in human skin, but wild horses will not drag from me the name of the owner. I have been asked what the cover looked like. I am sorry to say it looked very similar to pigskin.

One of the problems of the bookbinder is to bind a miniature book. Such a book I have by me at this moment. It is about the size of the nail on my little finger and weighs but 25 grains. This book is perfect in every way and is a triumph of the binder's skill.

Sometimes books are richly jewelled and studded with pearls, rubies, amethysts or diamonds. The stones may form either the design itself, or form centres from which the pattern springs. Very rich effects are thus obtained.

Of the curiosities, painting of the front edges of the book is the most charming. It is a matter of surprise that front edge painting is not seen more frequently. A favourite view or a scene mentioned in the text of the book can be painted on the edge in water colours. The painting can only be seen when the leaves are spread out. This beautiful art was brought to a fine degree by an English bookbinder named Edwards, when Queen Victoria first ascended the Throne. Many ladies are skilful with water colours, and most bookbinders can prepare the book for the artist.

I would like to tell you of the beauties of the bindings of the past; in Italy of Grolier, Maioli and Canevari, and in England of Queen Elizabeth, Mary Stuart and of that clever and brilliant prince, Henry, the son of James I, but time does not permit. Besides, that's another story.

APPENDIX D

Bookplates

At various times throughout its history the firm attempted to provide a complete service for collectors and librarians. Repair and conservation forming a natural corollary to the activities of a bookbinder; the early and apparently short-lived incursion into printing by Joseph Zaehnsdorf, in his first year of occupancy of the York Street premises, has been noted, as have the publishing and bookselling activities of the firm. There are some indications, of yet another ancillary service — that of providing bookplates. Advertisements in the *Bibliophile* of November 1908, and *Scribner's Magazine*, Christmas Number 1908, in addition to bookbinding and bookselling services, quoted the firm as 'designer of original bookplates'.

In the 1930s, the article on 'Symbolism in Bookbinding Design', in *The British and Colonial Printer and Stationer* for 22 December 1932, also mentioned bookplates as a method for personalizing a book. It showed two examples of bookplates, of no great merit, produced by Zaehnsdorfs, who were stated to be showing fresh enterprise in the design of bookplates.

No evidence has been found of Joseph Zaehnsdorf senior having a bookplate, but both his son and grandson had their own bookplates. These were a composite of two engravings by Jost Amman* showing sixteenth century bookbinders. The walls of the bindery and tools hanging thereon were taken from the woodcut of the bookbinder which was originally published in 1568, as one of the illustrations to a book of

---

* The sources of these illustrations are:
(a) Jost Amman and Hans Sachs. *Eygentliche Beschreibung Aller Stande auff Erden* . . . Frankfurt, 1586. A modern edition is, *The Book of Trades [Standebuch]*. Dover Publications, 1973.
(b) Jost Amman . . . *Charta Lusoria, Kunstliche und Wolgerissene Figuren, in ein new Kartenspiel* . . . Nurnberg, 1588.

Woodcut by Jost Amman, 1568

Bookplate for J. W. Zaehnsdorf

Opposite: Bookplate for E. J. W. Zaehnsdorf

Woodcut by Jost Amman, 1588

trades. The two figures of that illustration, using a plough and a sewing frame, were substituted by those from a later wood-cut, published in 1588. This second illustration is one of a series of playing cards from original designs by Jost Amman. One of the four suits of these cards is of books; the others being printer's ink dabbers, drinking vessels, and glass bowls. The bookbinder is the deuce, or second card, of the suit, as indicated by the numeral '2' at the top centre, and the two books. The figures on this cut are a binder using a beating hammer and a younger figure [apprentice?] at a sewing frame. It was this latter figure which was to appear on Zaehnsdorf advertisements and stationery for the last decade of the nineteenth century, and was also the basis of their medallic binder's mark, used as an additional signature on some of their finest exhibition bindings. The bookplate of J. W. Zaehnsdorf is illustrated — in the original the letter 'Z' and its background, and the outer border, are printed in red. The bookplate of Ernest Zaehnsdorf is similar, except that the single letter 'Z' is replaced by a monogram of 'EZ', and the German inscription is given in translation as, 'Safe Bind Safe Find'. Another family bookplate exists — the one which Ernest Zaehnsdorf produced for his wife, Gertrude.

Gertrude
Zaehnsdorf
her book

Acknowledgements

Thanks are due to Mr Tony Rainbird, Chairman of Zaehnsdorf Limited, for making available early records of the firm.
To Mr L. D. Watts, son of E. J. W. Zaehnsdorf and great-
grandson of Joseph Zaehnsdorf the founder of the firm, for the
loan of family photographs. To Mr Bernard Middleton and
the Rochester Institute of Technology, New York for sight of
the notebook in which Joseph Zaehnsdorf recorded information on his employees.

Useful assistance was received from Mr John Fuller.
Thanks are due to Miss E. Poyser, Archivist at Archbishop's
House, Westminster, for locating the Manning testimonial
volumes, and also to the staffs of the Victoria and Albert
Museum Library, the British Library, and particularly the
staffs of the St Bride Printing Library and the Guildhall
Library for their assistance on numerous occasions and never-
failing courtesy.

Index

TU/1